MASTERING MIND

*Dominants with Mental Illness
and Neurological Dysfunction*

MASTERING MIND

Dominants with Mental Illness
and Neurological Dysfunction

*Edited by Del Tashlin
and Raven Kaldera*

Alfred Press
Hubbardston, Massachusetts

Alfred Press
12 Simond Hill Road
Hubbardston, MA 01452

Mastering Mind: Dominants with Mental Illness and
Neurological Dysfunction
© 2014 by Del Tashlin and Raven Kaldera
ISBN 978-0-9905441-0-4

Cover Photography by John Riedell
Jawniffer Photography http://jawniffer.com/

Printed in cooperation with
Lulu Enterprises, Inc.
3101 Hillsborough St
Raleigh, NC 27607-5436

Dedicated to all the masters, mistresses, and dominants (and would-be masters, mistresses and dominants) out there who are afraid to admit they have problems, or ask for help.

It takes a lot of strength to keep from hiding.

Be strong, and know we care.

Contents

Foreword

This book is the fourth one in our series on power dynamic relationships and disability, and it was the hardest one to put together. Originally, I had actually wondered whether this book would ever be assembled. When I asked around the general BDSM demographic, my most frequent response was something along the lines of "People with mental illnesses shouldn't be in charge of another person! They can't even control themselves, and it wouldn't be safe."

It's true that someone in the middle of a violent psychotic break is not necessarily someone you want giving orders to others, and it's also true that the media is full of depictions of insane leaders doing awful things to their vulnerable followers. However, the reality is that there are quite a few dominant folk out there who are able to balance the trial of a glitchy brain/mind with protecting and caring for a submissive or slave, and while none of them would say that it is easy, their s-types seem to be quite happy—with both the treatment they give to the s-types and the strength they model in handling both challenges at the same time.

As we mentioned with our companion book, *Broken Toys*, no anthology is perfect and this one has plenty of holes. Because of the dearth of interviews and essays (even though the deadline was extended an extra year), this is a much slimmer volume than its companion, and very few mental illnesses and neurological problems are actually represented. It's hard enough to get dominant types to talk to you about their flaws and challenges—actually, getting dominant types to talk about anything is often like pulling teeth—and we were unable to find ones who were willing to talk much about challenges such as personality disorders. Many dominant types worried that even writing about these issues publicly in a book might give the impression that masters were sick people—a worry that they did not, interestingly enough, project onto Broken Toys, the companion volume for s-types. "Masters are seen as sinister enough," was the gist of their complaint. "We don't need to add to the problem by admitting that some of us actually have diagnoses."

What this book doesn't have, however, is horror stories from submissives and slaves, of which plenty filled my mailbox whenever I asked about these issues. These stories generally followed the outline of *Met master/mistress, they seemed so sane in the beginning. Then they began to act irrationally, and it all went bad. Later I decided that their actions sounded like they had Mental Problem X. They didn't believe it/refused to acknowledge it/would not get help for it. I'm now warning all submissives/slaves not to get involved with people who have Mental Problem X.*

Not only are we refusing to include such stories because they rarely (if ever) feature a clear diagnosis of the individual with the problem, we aren't including them because this is a book about how to do it right. The dominants, masters, and mistresses in this book are climbing the mountain against all odds, wrestling down the stubborn demons of trauma or neurochemistry or neurology, and figuring out how to do it all without damaging those most vulnerable to them. They may also be using their slave-resources as extra mental "limbs" to fill in where they fall down, or to help them manage the burdens of their disorders. If we never put out examples of how to do something right—even if most who try are failing—then we do nothing to help that failure rate.

Most especially, we do not provide anyone with hope that it can be done, and hope out in these areas is often in short supply. So is good advice from the people who've been there, and the loyal, intelligent subordinates who've been at their sides all the time. It may be that if the "horror stories" had been given hope and a road map drawn by peers, at least some of them might not have ended up horror stories. We hope to make this book such a light of hope and a road map of help. It is our gift to the future imperfect but brave dominants who will in turn teach the next generations.

RAVEN KALDERA
7/5/2014

Introduction: Stuck in the Middle
Del Tashlin

(This essay was also published in Broken Toys.*)*

The very first time I heard the mantra of the kink community—"Safe, Sane, Consensual"—I thought I was doomed to forever be excluded from their reindeer games. Oh, I understood the need for safety; the things we do are by their very nature dangerous and that is why we find them compelling and sexy. I also hold consent as Holy Writ due to some incidents in my past where consent was not sought or given. But the one in the middle—"sane"—there's just no definition of that word that I feel applies to me.

It started as casual conversation where I would ask for opinions on people with mental illness participating in the scene. The answers I got were pretty black and white—either the person felt that mental illness precluded you from ever experiencing sadomasochism or power dynamic relationships, or they themselves had a mental illness and understandably felt that it should not be an impediment to following one's sexual compass into the land of fetish, kink, and leather. There really was no grey area. Those who would exclude someone like me had a hard time conceptualizing any scenario where they felt comfortable with persons who were mentally ill being an active part of their leather families, kink organizations, or really in the community at all. They would almost always include some incredibly long and complicated story about people or couples who caused major rifts in the fabric of their community, or about those unfortunate souls who found themselves attracted to and involved with someone who treated them poorly and made them suffer for their love. Even when asked if there was ever a way for someone who had been diagnosed with a mental illness to overcome their symptoms or manage their behavior so as to be indistinguishable from anyone else, there was still trepidation and fear of a relapse or breakdown.

As persons with mental illness, we have to own some of that. Some of us have decided we no longer needed medication only to find that we really, really do. Others may not have accepted that we were truly sick, and were symptomatic in uncouth and hurtful ways until we came to grips with needing help. There are those who demand that anyone in their life must accept their "idiosyncrasies", whether that be memorizing the several personalities that come and go or bearing witness to repeated cycles of manic-depression because being manic made them feel energized and creative (and usually hypersexual, for a bonus). Even those who feel they are mostly in remission have break-outs when under undue stress or emotional upheaval. But what needs to be made clear about this is that everyone has bad days. How those bad days influence our behavior and whether or not that behavior demands abstaining from being a Master or slave, or even just being a Master or slave in public, that's where the grey area begins.

The ones who were open about their own mental illnesses told stories of how kink helped them heal, gave them new coping mechanisms, and allowed them a little freedom from the shame and isolation that commonly accompanies madness. From cutters who turned to ritualized needle play to reframe their coping mechanism into something beautiful and sexual rather than harmful and shameful, to Masters who were a grounding force when their submissive became manic, I not only heard their stories but became frustrated with that middle concept.

What does it really mean to be "sane"? Is the "sane" in "safe, sane, and consensual" really about the mental stability of those who find D/s attractive? I started asking respected presenters, educators, community leaders, and respected elders what is meant by "sane". Some gave it a very narrow focus that was less about the status of the players and more about indulging in fantasies that are tempered by the constraints of reality. An example given was from a well-known Leather Master/Educator who received requests from anonymous Internet seekers wanting a weekend-long scene culminating in the bottom getting murdered, for real. It wasn't so much his concern about whether the person making the request was mentally ill, as there are many who entertain mental fantasies about toeing the line between a really rough scene and permanent damage. Heck, the snuff film industry exists for a reason! But his real concern was the obviousness that these fantasies overlooked logistical concerns like evading law enforcement. I, myself, have been asked to enact scenes that carry consequences I was unwilling to accept in the name of desire. I am much more willing to accept the concept of sanity when it applies to actions rather than persons.

However, there were others who echoed the idea that there are some people who are just not centered enough even to watch the action in a play space or dungeon. The tales of people whose personality and/or actions became disruptive took on an epic level, including those who seemed to "prey" on a certain person/place/thing by moving from city to city once they had worn out their welcome. However much we're loath to admit it, most of us can think of someone we've met through our local munches, clubs, and parties that isn't playing with a full deck. But does that mean they should be expunged or shunned?

A common explanation for those who prefer the mantra "RACK" (Risk Aware Consensual Kink) over SSC is that many of the scenes you witness or perform in your bedroom or your preferred play space would look absolutely insane to a vanilla or non-kinky observer. The Crucible, the main play space in Washington, DC, hosts both BDSM and swinger events, and even offers separate membership cards for each crowd (even though they bestow the same benefits and can be used for either event type). This sometimes leads to a non-kinky swinger—usually one who learned about the club from the Internet—unwittingly finding themselves surrounded by acts us kinksters take for granted. One such incident I bore witness to was a middle-aged woman who had the wide-eyed stare of someone who had never even thought about BDSM before. She seemed relaxed at first, and just wandered around taking in all the different scenes on display. However, when an expert fire Top began lighting his torches and running them along a very willing bottom, the woman's demeanor changed dramatically. She started frantically looking for "someone in charge", because "that man is setting a woman on fire!"

Now it is time to focus on the topic of this book: the intersection of mental illness and power dynamics. Knowing that there are many M/s or D/s relationships that do not practice any form of kink, and some that don't consider themselves part of the Kink or Leather demographics, I still wanted to start from the concept of action rather than relationship. In a way, power dynamic relationships are a combination of several actions that create bonds and enforce the fantasy of being a Master or a slave. No matter how immersive your D/s or M/s relationship is, indentured servitude is (and will always be) illegal, even if the slave enthusiastically consents. So we rely on a variety of props, costumes, rituals and protocols to breathe life into our preferred way of relating. Most of those things might look as threatening as the fire torches to those who have not been exposed to or do not understand the desire for an unequal relationship.

However, as the following essays and personal stories will reveal, the ability to open up to your partners about your darkest sexual fantasies creates a pattern of communication that makes way for us to talk about other things that might embarrass or shame us. The ability to reinforce the dynamic while also supporting each other during times when coping skills alone aren't cutting it is one of the deepest magics I've witnessed in the M/s community. For Masters to admit that they aren't in control of their emotions a hundred percent of the time, or slaves to know it's expected for them to report any symptoms they may be experiencing without fear of judgment or retribution—these things bring color and complexity that asserts each relationship as functionally unique and powerful. After all, most slaves do not wish to submit to a faceless Master archetype who has no quirks, no need for assistance, no foibles that humanize them. Most masters do not expect slaves to be needless servants who perform sexual favors with the same expression they have for doing the laundry. We all want to find a collection of experiences, memories, outlooks, theories, behaviors, and desires that will continue to enthrall and intrigue us for decades.

To me, there is nothing more sane than wanting and creating a deeply emotional and meaningful relationship where the partners involved support and comfort each other on good days and bad—a relationship where we can take off our public face and be a little dysfunctional without fear or shame. Finding people who care enough to learn when we need a little alone time and when we need to be dragged out of our caves kicking and screaming. Having someone create unusually sexy ways to remind us to take our meds, or write in our journals, or to call our therapists. Honestly, I think the idea of a "sane person" is an unobtainable ideal anyway, if what we mean is "free from emotional distress or chemical imbalances". My idea of a "sane person" is "one who has figured out how to relate to the world with as little distress as possible." And the people who are about to share their stories with you are just that.

I hope you find a treasure trove of ideas, concepts, and structures that will help you enrich your own relationships or help discern the right relationships in the future. I also hope that you recognize a little bit of yourself, your lovers, your friends, your family, and so on, in these stories, to prove that none of us are as "sane" as we think we are. If we deny entry to the world of power dynamics based on sanity, only the ones who fail to recognize their insanity will get to play.

> *The one man in the world who never believes he's*
> *mad is the madman.*
> –L. Ron Hubbard

DEL A. TASHLIN
6/18/2014

Sky's Height To Underworld:
Mood Disorders

Interview with Jawn
Jawn (with help from Jawn's Doll)

This is a two-part interview with a master/slave couple who both cope with mental illnesses. Jawn's interview is here, while the interview for his slave, Jawn's Doll, is in our book on subs and slaves with mental illnesses.

Jawn:

I was in the Air Force for twenty years until I retired for reasons of mental health, and I have a fifty per cent disability rating from the veterans administration for depression. What triggered the depression was the death of my second wife, with whom I had a very close and intense relationship. My first marriage was pretty miserable for both of us, and for the first time I'd met someone who was amazing—a good communicator, sexy, good-looking, loving, and a submissive. We were only together for three years when I came home one day for lunch and found her. I thought that she was napping at first, but she had had an aneurysm and had passed. Sarah died February 15, 2005.

I'd already had a tendency throughout my life to be a gloomy person, but I hadn't connected that to depression. I'd had some awful things happen to me before that. My father abused me physically and sexually. My mother fell asleep at the wheel and drove off the road when I was nine years old and died; my grandmother, who was a terrible person, told me out of anger and spite that she must have been drunk. During my teen years, I got into heroin and was a junkie for a couple of years. I've been clean for more than two decades now, though. I got clean and went into the military.

Then, during my first marriage, our first child was born prematurely, at twenty-two weeks, weighing only ten ounces. He lived for four hours and I held him in my arms before he died. My first marriage was fifteen years, and it was no fun for either of us. It felt like my life was just one bad thing after another, and then finally with my second marriage I got a taste of real happiness for the first time ... and then it was snatched away when she died suddenly. It was like the Universe was mocking me, as if it had given me a taste of what it was like to be content, and then taken it.

At first my therapist said that my condition was simple bereavement, but then I just kept getting worse. At first, after her death, I was running on inertia. When you lose someone you love, something in your head keeps saying, "Oh, yeah, they'll be back any time now," even though you know intellectually that they are gone. I think that the hardest part is when the rest of you catches up to reality some months later. At that point, people are expecting you to be getting over it, and they aren't asking you if you're OK any more. I really missed her a lot; it was like the rug was just yanked right out from under me. I took it really hard.

I had an Air Force therapist the remaining time I was in the Air Force—I was surprised, looking back, and overall very pleased, with the quality of therapy that I got from that therapist. I didn't feel that there was anything I couldn't talk about with her, but the depression just got worse and worse. I started feeling like there was no point in going on. I went through a phase for a few months of wanting to quit life and join her. But I did have three kids, and I didn't feel like it would be morally right of me to abandon them, so I didn't have that option. I was tempted, but I kept myself alive and going on.

While it started out as grief, I think that being sad for so long changed my body chemistry and became clinical depression. For a very long time I really didn't have my mojo. I got out of bed, and I did whatever minimum work I could do for the Air Force that would keep me from getting in trouble, and I dealt with the kids as best I could, and then I went to bed. I went through the motions, but it was very hard. My co-workers were resentful and mocking; they felt like I was lazy and malingering, and they called me a loser. I was an enlisted flyer, but when I told my therapist that I had suicidal ideation, I was disqualified so that I wouldn't take a plane and dive it into the side of a mountain, and maybe take a bunch of people with me. So being honest with them ruined my career, and I ended up in a boring office job, but I don't resent that—I was getting the care I needed.

I retired from the Air Force in March of 2007. They tried a whole variety of medications on me, but all of them had undesirable side effects, especially sexual side effects. I could get turned on, but I couldn't orgasm, and that was even more depressing. So I've decided against medication, at least for now, but if I were to start wanting to kill myself, I would go right back in and get on meds.

Currently I'm doing better than I have been since my wife died, but the depression still comes and goes. It's seasonal, and certain dates and anniversaries can really put me in a slump. Between November 6, which is my anniversary with Sarah, and February 15 when she died, it's at its worst. April 7 is the date that my son died, so I get a little down around then as well. When I wake up depressed, I feel scattered and less creative. Overall I feel less focused than I did before I fell into the depression, so I think something really changed in my brain. I have a little home business doing photography, and on some days I have the energy to do the PhotoShopping or go out and take pictures, and some days I don't. I manage my depression on the bad days by making myself do something anyway, whether that's to sweep my studio or organize my files.

I make myself get up in the morning and get dressed, and I have a variety of coping mechanisms that help me feel better, like going outside for a walk every day to take pictures. If I spend time outside, it helps keep me on track. If I were to let myself lay in bed until noontime … well, my head would say, "That laying-in-bed-all-day thing was pretty good, I think I'll do that again," and it would go downhill from there.

Jawn's Doll:

We email back and forth from my work in the morning, and those mornings when he sleeps in, I sometimes get a little nervous. Usually he's physically ill when that happens, though, with a cold or something.

Jawn:

While you can't push mental illness away by force of will, the kind of willpower that it takes for me to make myself get up and get dressed and do the coping mechanisms that help, that comes from the same will that makes me a good master. One of my core beliefs is avoiding hypocrisy. When I tell my slavegirl, "When I say that you do something, you do it," I would be a hypocrite if I wasn't putting the same amount of effort into my life. Of course I'm not putting down people who are so depressed that they can't get out of bed, because I've been there, and just knowing that you can't get out of bed makes you feel even worse. "I can't get out of bed, and I'm the biggest loser ever." It's really hard to dig your way out from that, so my policy is to avoid going there if it's at all possible. So if I'm going to be telling her to do something, I'm not going to be the kind of person who lets myself be pushed around by an illness and just lays down for it. I'm going to do what I have to do to keep it under control.

My doll and I met October 20th, 2007. I know that was our first date because all my photos are organized by date, so I can remember it. We'd exchanged messages on collarme.com—you can actually find good people on collarme, contrary to popular belief. Our first date was at the Worcester art museum, in public to make sure that no one was too crazy. At first she just bottomed to me; she would come over once a week and we would have kinky fun-time. There was an immediate attraction; neither of us intended to have sex on the first date, but she was so responsive that she was having orgasms while we made out, so perhaps that counts as sex. She was looking for someone older than her, and I was actually about the youngest guy that she was willing to consider at the time.

Jawn's Doll:
I don't see anyone younger than me as someone that I can follow. I was seeing a life experience gap with people under a certain age; if I was telling them, "No, this is how things work, because I've been there," I couldn't submit to that. If I'm telling them how life works, why are they telling me what to do? But my master has seen a whole lot of life, not all of it pleasant, and he knows how to react to hard times. He's been through a lot, and that made me respect him more.

He told me pretty early in our relationship about everything that had happened to him. One of our first agreements was that we were going to be totally open and honest with each other. We met at the end of October, which was leading into his seasonal depression, so we had to talk about it fairly soon.

Jawn:

I wouldn't tell someone that I just met everything about myself—and in fact, when someone I've just met tells me everything about themselves, if kind of puts me off—but you can tell when people are ready for information. It went quickly with her, but there was a progression of information as I learned more about her, and learned I could trust her. I wasn't going to tell her about my father's abuse of me, for instance, in the beginning. I want sympathy, but not pity, so I'm not going to open up right away.

Jawn's Doll:

He only told me recently, for example, how his mother died. That's when I realized why Jawn had given me orders that if I'm ever driving at night and I get sleepy, he wants me to pull off the road and find a hotel. That's a really good rule, but I only recently found out where it was coming from.

Jawn:

She is my little treasure, my little court jester, my little ray of sunshine. One of the reasons that I took her on was because she is so positive. When I see personal ads online saying things like "I'm a worthless slave, keep me in the basement," I think, "Why would I want that? I'm gloomy enough as it is, I want someone cheerful!" Although sometimes when I'm feeling bad, her cheerfulness is actually kind of annoying, and she's good about dialing it back when I need quiet.

While my doll never knew me during my junkie era, one of her standing orders is that if I start using heroin, she is to take everything and get out. I don't believe that I'm ever going to do that again, but I can't turn my back on that possibility. So the rule is that she is required to do everything that Clean Jawn says without question, and if Using Jawn ever shows up again, she is not to listen to anything he says, and has to get the hell out of Dodge, because Clean Jawn said so.

Jawn's Doll:

Helping him with his depression is an interesting tightrope to walk, because I've got my own anxiety issues as well. When he's feeling like he's not up to top standards, I have to be understanding that he's not going to be as focused on me as I might want. I'll try to help however I can. For example, we're starting up a photography business, and we have a couple of photography blogs. I do all the site maintenance, and he wants me to help him upload two posts a week on this blog, and three posts a week on that blog. So he'll send me a bunch of photos to upload, and sometimes I'll notice that I've gone through all the pictures and no more are coming in. Then I'll start checking in on him, and gently reminding him, "There's this job that you gave me to do, but I need you to do something before I can do my part, so what should I do now?" I don't worry about it all that much any more; I just know that it's time to do more checking in.

Jawn:

I don't like to mention it to her, especially when it's about my second wife, because I don't want it to feel like a slap in the face to her—"Oh, my dear departed spouse, how saintly she was, she can do no wrong, I've idealized her..." I don't want to pull that on my doll, because that would just be bullshit.

Sometimes, when I'm having a bad day, I feel overwhelmed and I don't know what to do. During those times, I see all the negative things about my pictures— someone could tell me that this was a great picture, and while I'm appreciative, all I can see is the five different ways in which it's not a great picture. When I'm feeling better, I can remind myself that not every picture is going to be good, or the light was terrible, and I just had an off day, and it's no big deal. Whereas when I'm feeling depressed, I feel like I can't create, and if I can't create why should I go on trying? Every little thing is huge, and I think, "What kind of fucking photographer am I?"

Jawn's Doll:

Obviously, I think he's wonderful and amazing. But sometimes, like last week, we did portrait photography and it wasn't exactly under great working conditions. Then he was looking at all the photos and saying how he couldn't find a single good picture of anybody, and it was my job to point out, "No, look, this one isn't so bad, and this one is nice in this way," and give him an alternate viewpoint to counteract it.

Jawn:

I know that it's not exactly true when I feel like that—for example, the people in those pictures are raving about them—and I do listen to my doll. I know that she has good judgment, and I trust her. I can ask her opinion, and while she might be wrong, she's usually got a good take on things. If she doesn't know, she'll say so. She does like to present every option to me, so that she feels like her ass is covered, but I tell her, "Don't be afraid to fail. Don't be afraid to say something wrong." I want another eye on things. Her honest feedback is important, and it's not to be punished but to be rewarded, no matter what she says. Sometimes she can be kind of a teacher's pet, and I have to say, "Stop sucking up and tell me what you think."

I agree on principle that if you're in a certain space, you should probably refrain from making major decisions. I'm very rarely there any more, fortunately. If you're in bad shape, don't do any heavy lifting with the brain during those times. But I take a very rational approach; I'm into finding the best way to do things, and I don't have to be the one who thought of it in order for it to be the best way. I'm always open to hearing ideas from her as to how things could work better.

If I could give advice to would-be masters who live under the gray cloud and are wondering if they could do the job, I'd say that you first need to figure out how to manage your own illness. For some people, that's going to be taking their medication when they need to. For others, it will be a regimen of non-medicinal things to help keep you on track, like "I will go for a walk every day. I will play my guitar twice a week. I'm not going to stay up past two or be in bed after eight. I'm going to put this much time and effort into my work." Those are investments you make to keep you from sliding down. Therapists can help you figure out useful things to do. Don't just make up rules for the sake of having rules; actually experiment and figure out what works, which will be different for every person. If something unforeseen happens in your life, you may not be able to keep to your helpful activities, so have contingency plans in case of those situations.

And if you do have a sub or a slave, that's another tool for you to use to keep yourself on track. I've gained her trust, so she isn't sitting around pleading, "Don't kill yourself, I need you!" But I've taught her how to encourage me to do the things I need to do. One useful trait that might be helpful in a slave might be being good at scheduling things, and organizing. Doing my creative work really helps me, and having her take care of the organizing—getting things up on the web and such—is very helpful. I want to be productive, I want to work as much as I can, and she makes it easier for me. It's good that I can count on her to be there to support me in doing as much as I can.

Jawn's Doll:

There are also certain things that he wants to happen around the house, because it takes stress off of him to know that they are being done. For example, there should always be clean clothes, and certain things should appear in the way he wants them done. Sometimes he'll good-naturedly pick on me and say, "Oh, the laundress is falling behind! I don't have any clean underwear." And then the laundress gets very upset and gets to it.

My harsh real advice to a would-be sub is that if you don't think you can handle a master who has major depressive episodes, be completely honest with that master and tell them that this is something that you don't know that you can do. Don't just stop returning emails or telling them passive-aggressively that you're just busy. It's totally not a failure to say, "You are a little more than I can handle." It's so much easier for everyone in the long run to just say that you're not cut out for it.

My ex-husband also had depressive moments, but he would just retreat and not talk to me. Jawn is honest and open with me, and just says, "I'm not feeling that great today," so I always know where things stand. The fact that he was so open and honest with what was going on with him—he might not have told me every little detail, but he told me as much as I needed to hear at that time—kept me from having a lot of trust issues with him. That was the most important thing for me. It wasn't ever something that he sprang on me without warning.

Jawn:

That's because I hate hypocrisy so much. It's like I've told her: I don't want to learn at the last minute that you've been keeping a problem from me. I don't want to learn about something on the Internet that you haven't told me first. That was our first big argument, actually, but she's been really good about it ever since. She doesn't make the same mistake twice, and honesty and openness are so important in surviving this.

Jawn's Doll:

I'd advise a sub in this situation to actively look for things that you can do to help. But check them first—if you aren't sure that something will help, ask! And don't stop treating your master like a master. Sometimes when I see that he's not doing so well, I will be more hesitant to bring him difficult questions or come to him with my issues. But eventually I've learned that doesn't help either of us or our relationship. I need to bring things to him anyway, because that's holding up my end of the deal to be open and honest.

Jawn:

But a sub also has to be respectful about how they ask. One of the things that took me aback at first was that she was always asking me, "How are you doing?" That was a problem for me, because I was suspicious of that—"I'm fine, why are you asking? Are you getting ready to give me bad news or something? What, you want a status report out of me or something?" No, I'm the one who asks you for a status report; if you want information about me, you're going to have to approach it properly. But then I met her mother and her father and they say "How are you doing?" every time there's a lull in conversation. It's their cultural thing. So that's not so bad.

A sub has to learn how to get information about their master's moods in a way that doesn't sound like they're your mom or your parole officer—"You're not thinking of cutting your wrists or doing some heroin today, are you?" It has to remain respectful.

Jawn's Doll:

This is how I get a bead on the day's situation. When I get to work in the morning I send him a quick email telling him that I love him, or some other little thing. Then he'll write back and tell me that he loves me too. Then I'll message again with something like, "So how are you feeling this fine morning?" I keep it light and a little flippant, not serious, so as to entertain him, and he'll tell me. Generally when he's still in bed, it's because he's got a cold or flu.

Jawn:

When I'm in bed with a flu, I like to give her all the awful details, because I know it will gross her out, and I'll get some kind of sadistic enjoyment out of it. But we did have an argument in the beginning when she would get worried if I didn't email her back, and she would be upset. So I had to make it clear to her that every email from me is a gift, and she should be grateful to get each one, and she shouldn't be timing them. If something is wrong, I will tell her. That's the kind of controlling behavior that you have to root out of a sub as quickly as possible, and when you hear how they were upset because you didn't email them back right away, you have to be blunt and say, "Well, I was just doing whatever I wanted to at the time ... which apparently wasn't emailing you. And that's how our relationship is supposed to work, remember?"

Being Manic Depressive and Being M/s
Das

I've titled this essay "Being" Manic Depressive, because there is a fundamental correlation between "being" and "manic-depression" that is not well understood, particularly in the psychiatric and psychological communities.

We are, all of us, always in a mood. Even that vague lack of any particular mood that we often find ourselves in is not in itself a lack, but a positive determination of ourselves as "just so-so", "ok but not great". When we ask someone how they are, in a sincere way, we mean the same as "what is your current mood". Mood discloses, at any given time, how we are as a whole, our state of being, which is not disclosed via any other means. This means that moods and emotions are not directly related, and although mood does affect emotional response, in itself it is not a response. Emotions are, on the other hand, a response to particular things, events and people within the world. Conflating them as affects gets in the way of any real understanding of what a mood disorder is.

It should be obvious that changes in our state of being affect how we experience and respond to concrete events and things in the world. What is often missed is that a given mood often occurs without any prompting from events and things in the world. When moods are more extreme, and change more rapidly, this becomes radically obvious in a way that it rarely does for most people. It results in significantly inappropriate responses, for example, to specific events, people, or situations. But since we are always already in a mood, by the time we try to control that mood it is already too late, and this temporal discrepancy that makes moods difficult to handle is exacerbated severely when they are both extreme and change rapidly. Since being with others is a complex combination of people, events and situations, being with others is bound to be a different proposition in some ways for those with bipolar disorder.

There is a further complication—moods are contagious. While they are contagious to a degree in any case, those with extreme moods inflict them to a greater degree on others, and simultaneously are more affected by others' moods. This leads to our particular situation, where both Master and slave are manic depressive.

I'm a 45-year-old (mostly) straight white male, English by birth, Canadian by upbringing and I'm in an M/s relationship with a 39-year-old (mostly) straight (mostly) black woman from North Carolina. I'm relatively well-educated, having been a Jesuit seminarian prior to studies in secular philosophy, mass communications and mathematics. My activities over my life so far have ranged from playing soccer at a competitive level to being the lead singer in an electronica band to being a software architect for the Department of Defense. I've been diagnosed as manic depressive long enough that it was still called manic depression at the time, and I see no reason to change it. I sometimes refer to manic-depression as the most amusing medical condition there is, since I don't know of any other medical conditions where things like hypersexuality and a compulsion to shop are common symptoms, and less usual ones include investing in personal submarines.

I've been in the BDSM scene seemingly forever; I went to a fetish dance show when I was fourteen and have been involved in one way or another since. I didn't get involved in M/s specifically until my mid-thirties, having tried unsuccessfully to navigate egalitarian relationships with rather dominant women, including an ill-fated marriage to a vampire dominatrix.

My issues affect my self-perception indirectly, in the sense that my self-perceptions require more validation and more testing against reality than I think most people find necessary. I have been doing that my whole life, though, as a necessary coping mechanism, even prior to being diagnosed. In terms of "wanting to be the dominant" in the relationship, it's a strange phrasing to me—I am the dominant partner, and I have been in all my relationships. It was more a matter of admitting that I couldn't help being that, and going with it rather than trying unsuccessfully to counter it.

My slave and I have been together for seven years. Initially we started in a quad with our former partners, both of whom wanted to be polyamourous. Although that was never particularly our thing, we went along with it until it ceased to work for various reasons. We're still good friends with my slave's ex, but the relationship with my ex (which was also M/s, while my slave's wasn't) ended rather more explosively and we haven't spoken in a couple of years.

For me M/s is an extreme way of being together. That suits me as a manic depressive because it is aligned with my tendencies elsewhere which are similarly extreme. The most difficult aspect of being a Master as a manic depressive is ensuring the appropriateness of my actions and responses, since an extreme mood can result in an inappropriately overwhelming or underwhelming response to a given event. Much of our being together is based on the notion of place, and the appropriateness with which we are in our respective places and thereby maintain the household and each other's place in it. As a result, the propriety of what I do (within our own parameters) is crucial, and at times challenging. During a very severe depression once I did get to the point of feeling that I couldn't maintain the situation, but luckily I received sufficient support from my slave that we were able to get through it and continue together.

With regard to decisions, the reality is I won't always get it right, but then neither will anyone else. I do try to leave decisions that don't have to be made in that moment long enough that I can assess the options in more than one mood. My slave does raise questions when things seem very "off", though she doesn't disobey no matter what the decision. The flip side is that I don't avoid taking responsibility for bad decisions no matter what mood they were made in. Our relationship is about control, and I control things whether or not the way I do it is always the "best" way, which is impossible to fully determine in any case.

Many people in the bipolar community recommend against bipolars being intimate with one another because (as noted above) the effect they have on each other will be more extreme, which can lead to mood spiralling, both upwards and downwards. The difficulty with this is that people want intimate relationships with those that they feel understand them, and in our situation very few non-bipolars have a natural understanding of how we experience things. In an M/s situation particularly, that understanding is crucial if the Master wants to control his or her slave in a manner worthy of the name and not behave as an absentee landlord.

In any case, every woman I've been with has ended up being diagnosed sooner or later as bipolar—I am more attracted to those I relate to in a basic way (and being bipolar is a basic way of being), whether I know that they are bipolar to begin with, or they even know it.

When we first got together my ex and I were both diagnosed, but my current slave was not. As we got more intimate, I saw fairly obvious symptoms in her which were making work difficult to deal with (and working was making her symptoms more difficult to deal with). Once she had seen a psychiatrist and been very quickly diagnosed, she went on the usual med merry-go-round until she found a regimen that agreed with her in terms of the balance of controlling the worst symptoms without having worse side effects. She also went through the "psychiatrist merry-go-round", which I was also going through due to having recently moved to the area. Once we found a reasonably competent practitioner (no easy feat sometimes), she also applied for permanent disability. She had not been working for a couple of years by that point, since I didn't think it was doing her well, and she was awarded disability without so much as a question from SSDI. Personally I think the trail of economic destruction she had left behind at various jobs convinced them it was in everybody's interest that she not work. Since she became an at-home slave, her stress levels have dropped significantly, which slows the mood swings and mollifies them somewhat. In combination with a reasonable regimen of medication she can be termed "stable", although non manic-depressives should realize that "stable" is always relative to the extremes of manic-depression—a "stable" manic-depressive is generally still extreme by the standards of non manic-depressives.

I am the opposite when it comes to working and being manic-depressive. Working is somewhat stabilizing for me, although people around me have tended to overstate how stabilizing it is, since the causality chain is stronger from being unstable to having work issues than the other way around. Part of the odd reality of being manic depressive, at least partially due to its contagious nature, is that reality appears in many ways to follow the mood one happens to be in. If I'm in a hypomanic or manic state I can convince just about anyone of just about anything, which means I'm not going to find it difficult finding a contract, whereas if I'm depressed, the phone doesn't even ring. One of the benefits of working in the software industry is that much of the most interesting work is contract, and as a result I've been able to do interesting work without much questioning regarding the time gaps in my resume. Of course, the other major benefit is earning a sufficiently high pay rate to cover those gaps and to allow myself the luxury of a stay at home slave. I do best in a state of mild hypomania, and I balance the medications to the finest degree I can to maintain that state.

The hypersexuality I experience as part of mania and hypomania is also contagious, and it's damnably difficult containing my own hypersexuality when it rubs off on everyone around me, making sex the most available thing imaginable. When it's combined with the adrenaline rush of being sadistic it can be very difficult to control, which is part of the reason I rarely play with other submissives. While I could both play and have sex with them, having sex is not necessarily something I want to do with just anybody, but in a moment doubly fueled by hypersexuality and adrenaline it might be difficult to avoid. For the time being, since the breakup with my ex, we have been living as a monogamous M/s couple, partly due to the reality of the above and partly because I find the politics involved in any poly situation irritating. Once there are more than two people in a situation it becomes inherently political, because anything said or done to or with one person can be taken differently by the other, and it requires a constant self-checking of one's polity to ensure everyone takes everything the way it was intended. Of course this can happen situationally with friends as well as additional lovers, but in the latter case it becomes almost inevitable. My slave is monogamous in any case, both by predilection and by order.

My slave and I live with being manic depressive and being with another manic depressive, and honestly we love it. We have been lucky enough to be aware of ourselves and how we respond, have decent coping mechanisms to avoid some of the worse issues that can arise, and give the other a place to be who we are with understanding. We are extreme—our extreme moods don't come from nowhere;

they are the disclosure of the reality that we are extreme. Our relationship, as an M/s couple, is likewise extreme by most people's standards. It suits us fine. Being extreme isn't necessarily better or worse, but the added danger can give an added spice.

We avoid spiralling each other as best we can by checking our moods versus what is actually happening, checking our own responses and the other's responses against evidential reality, and doing our best to balance and counter inappropriate moods. It works for us because we actively maintain it: countering overreactions in the other with underreactions in ourselves or vice versa—validating responses without necessarily agreeing that the reason for the response is valid. We both have a multitude of coping mechanisms that are also effective on the other when their own aren't sufficient. Some would see it as a bit of a high-wire act, but as the leader of a famous acrobatic troupe once said, "Life is when you're up on the wire, the rest is just waiting around."

Mastering Bipolar and More

Master Fire (with help from slave elliot)

Master Fire:

Our name is Master Fire, and We are the head of an M/s household affectionately known as "The House of Fire". We have had multiple members in our household in the past, but at the time of this writing, slave elliot is Our only slave. This slave has been collared for three years, and We have lived together for almost two, which began when we moved across the country for Our job. But first, a note about the pronouns in this essay: Our M/s relationships are spiritually driven and Our odd speech protocols are guided by our spiritual beliefs. We use the "royal We" form of speech while the slaves use "it". In this manner, no one in the household uses the egoic "I". While SM and sex are a great deal of fun and We enjoy having those in an M/s relationship when they happen, the dynamic isn't based on, and may not even contain, either. With slave elliot, We do not have a romantic or sexual relationship, due to the fact that our sexual orientations don't match. We are a straight woman and it is a gay man.

Our own unique set of diagnoses include Type II Bipolar Disorder, ADD and Anxiety with, in Our opinion, an undiagnosed case of OCD and a somewhat problematic undiagnosed case of dyslexia. We treat the diagnosed disorders with a combination of Western medicine, natural health care, and behavior awareness/modification, with emphasis heavy on the latter two. There are two important points about the success of Our treatment regime. First, We have never stopped taking Our treatments just because We feel better. This is a common problem in the treatment of Bipolar patients, and so We mention it specifically. Two, We have developed a good sense of self awareness through the behavioral awareness techniques, so that We often know We are swinging when We are experiencing it. In addition, elliot is under orders to gently point it out if We don't simply announce it first.

To give more details about it: Our combination of disorders currently manifestx as fairly mild manic swings and somewhat more intense depressive swings. Irritability, a low frustration threshold, and a quick temper seem to be the three overarching symptoms that manifest all the time. These are mostly controlled by behavioral modification, though We haven't quite mastered the technique of catching them completely before they outwardly manifest. The outward manifestation is, however, much less obvious than what actually goes on inside Our head. Probably the worst behavior that We can't seem to get under control, even though We take steps to do so, is the occasional time where We will take the wrong meds—meaning that We will take the night meds in the morning or vice versa. We lay out Our meds two weeks at a time, night and morning in separate colored and labeled containers, yet still manage to take the wrong set. We find this extremely frustrating and are convinced it must be some manifestation of dyslexia, or perhaps a side effect of one of the medicines We take.

The manic swings mostly consist of lots of physical energy, talking a great deal very quickly, and being extroverted in very "bubbly", happy way. If this persists, it can lead to insomnia, the desire to shop, and sometimes hypersexuality. When We swing manic, We make sure to Take Our Meds and tweak the natural remedies. This involves taking more of the things that help Us sleep and help create a sense of calm, and perhaps less of the things that gives Us energy. We also, when needed, employ relaxing and grounding activities such as meditation.

The depression, which occurs more frequently, manifests as being tired and silent, wanting to be left alone, and sleeping a lot. Our mind-to-mouth filter will often function less, though not often to the point of doing what We consider to be real damage to others. We are introverted and have a tendency to cancel outside plans and call in sick to work to stay in Our "cave". Depressive episodes seem to be linked by being overworked and not sleeping well. This is why, for Us, a manic phase often triggers the opposite mood swing because of the insomnia. It doesn't seem to be the case that a depressive swing will spontaneously trigger a manic swing, however. Our depressive swings seem to be lower than the manics are high. In order to counter the depressive swing, We will modify the natural remedies, get plenty of rest and sometimes go out and do something fun even though We'd rather stay home. The grounding and meditation can help here, too, as those things work to return Us to a balance point on Our scale. When We feel Ourself experiencing of a weak mind-to-mouth filter, We make a point of just staying home and limiting interaction with people, even if going out might be a good idea.

We are blessed to have a slave who has very similar diagnoses, with a high sense of self awareness about its own moods. We feel this makes it much more able to handle Our swings. Our slave also has the emotional intelligence required to understand that if We behave in a less than optimal manner, it isn't a reflection of its worth or how We really feel about it, but a manifestation of the disorders. We have ordered elliot to disobey any orders that obviously come from a place that does not offer good stewardship; for example if we were to become extremely unbalanced. We feel comfortable knowing that elliot could make a decision about Our health, and do what is necessary in order to get Us treatment if We were not mentally able to do that for Ourself. This has never happened, nor do We hope it ever will, but we trust elliot's judgement about what is and isn't a place of good stewardship.

Even given all that, it is the low frustration threshold mixed with the expectations that come out of the OCD that seem to affect our dynamic the most, in Our opinion. We have a picture in Our head of how things should be organized, be that physical placement of items, expectation of orders, or needing and following plans. The biggest clashes have been over the expectation of order in the apartment. Disarray frustrates Us. We have learned to be somewhat compassionate with Ourself about Our own pockets of disarray (Our desk, which is the kitchen table at the moment, always seems to be covered with various things), but Our frustration at disarray elsewhere is a challenge. Since part of elliot's duties include domestic service, when its progress deviates from Our OCD expectations, We feel very frustrated. It took a lot for Us to realize that elliot simply cannot function at the level which Our expectations require. To this day, We can't bring Ourself to understand why not, but we work to accept that it "just is".

The two of Us have had to compromise in this area; elliot does its best and makes an effort to keep the main areas more tidy than it otherwise would, though We constantly order it to put things away (which frustrates both of us). We also continually attempt to relax Our expectations, and have allowed it to keep its own bedroom at a level of chaos that seems to make it happy. When Our frustration level gets high, which is usually when We are experiencing anxiety or a manic swing, We will start cleaning, putting things away, and ordering it to pick stuff up off the floor of its bedroom. On occasion, We have had to simply shut its bedroom door so as not to see the mess. There are a lot of challenging emotions wrapped up in this area. We think elliot appreciates the effort We put into being calm about this, though We aren't entirely sure it knows how much effort it takes. We feel that it doesn't understand Our compulsions in this area any more than We understand its lack of desire for things to have order. Both of us, however, know that neither of us has to understand it to be compassionate toward it and do our best. This is all that We require.

slave elliott:

This slave agrees about the above dynamic as its Master has expressed. The most frustrating parts with regard to its Master's temperaments are those days when we are not on the same "wavelength". She will say something, and it will make an agreeing and supportive statement, then its Master will argue with its supposed inaccuracies, and after several minutes of debate we both realize in frustration that we've been arguing the same side of the argument just using different language or seeing it from a slightly different perspective. Whenever its Master has those days of being irritated by everything, it is able to disengage its questioning of what it may have done or not done. Sometimes its Master's energies are so opposite to its own that it just gives Her space and doesn't take on Her energies in a personal way. However, while such days exist, they are rare, and tend to be exacerbated by either of us working too much, sleeping too little, or sometimes spending too much time together for many days in a row. Fortunately when one of us is out of sorts, the other is usually more stable at the time. It is rare that we are both lacking in mood stability simultaneously.

This slave feels that Master Fire has a good handle on Her own challenges with regard to Her mental health. This slave mostly uses patience, acceptance, and remaining dispassionate to keep from being overly affected by its Master's symptoms when they happen, although it will sometimes ask Her questions to point out any symptoms She may be unaware of. However, it allows Her to decide, so it is never phrased as an accusation or similar statement. This slave is aware that it might not be interpreting the behavior appropriately, but after the time we have spent together, it is more often accurate these days. We both strive to keep ourselves in check and have each other to fall back on in the event that our own checks and balances fail. They have yet to do so, and we have never needed to give one another more than a gentle nudge by pointing out something the other is overlooking. This is how we maintain our M/s in the face of these challenges—not by striving to live up to unrealistic ideals, but by working with who we actually are, and using that to mold a cohesive household. The shape of our relationship may be irregular compared to much of the M/s dynamics it has seen, but it is functional and seems to fit us well. Above all else, we share a love and compassion for one another, perhaps even on a level that one affected with bipolar cannot have with someone who doesn't understand the experience of it.

Finding The Capability Within Your Relationship, Part II

Daddy T

(Part I of this interview was published in Kneeling In Spirit: Disabled Submissives.*)*

A bit of an introduction first: I am known as Daddy_T or KnightHawk in the scene. I have been a switch in the past; however, after my last relationship where I was a collared submissive, I realized that I am better suited for being a Dominant. This is partly because this relationship, like every other relationship that I had chosen to enter into as the submissive, turned out to be very unhealthy. But when I am the Dominant within a relationship, the relationship tends to last longer and be healthier. I have been in this lifestyle called BDSM/Leather for 20-some-odd years. At the age of 44, I have now earned the title of Master, and have been honored with this title by my collared slave and pet.

If I think about where my inability to choose a healthy relationship as a submissive comes from, I find that it goes back to when I was young. I was actually introduced into this lifestyle at the age of six by my father's third wife. There were no sexual relations, but I called her Mistress and was her slave in a very unhealthy manner. This is also where a lot of my emotional disabilities came from, according to my doctors.

I have Obsessive-Compulsive Disorder and Bipolar Disorder, so living with me is not always easy. My slave calls herself lil bobbins, and that's what I'll call her here. She has her own physical disabilities, so we take care of each other. I talked about my physical disabilities in *Hell On Wheels*, and they are why I am on disability. My slave has adapted herself very well to finding ways to make my life easier in spite of my mental illnesses. I started out as a mentor and play partner for her, and then later I was gifted by her choice to offer me her collar. Since then, we have been working slowly due to her disabilities and mine. I am a very positive-minded person, so I teach her to be as well.

She is very good with finances, so I let her handle the finances of our household. We work out the chores so that I get a clean house and my OCD is not going nuts, but lil bobbins gets to rest since she is the one working outside the house in a 9 to 5 job. I clean the bathroom, because with her back injury that would cause her too much pain, whereas I have learned to block my pain out. She does the dishes because with my OCD I would be in there re-washing them every few minutes and wasting dish soap and still not doing a good job. (I've been told that I am horrible at doing dishes.) I vacuum because that way I am not going back over everything she has already vacuumed a hundred times with a fine-toothed comb. In a trade-off, she does the laundry because she has specific ways of wanting it done and won't freak out if I sort it my way and do it.

We recently worked out a new system that I am putting into play. We both have memory problems; mine are due to my bi-polar and hers are due to stress, DID, and one of her medications. There are certain aspects of chores that she keeps forgetting, which gets her in trouble. To work this out, I am writing out notes to post around the house to remind her of the details she typically forgets. This way we don't have to go over the same things repeatedly, and with the notes posted around for her to see I'll know it is not her medicine or the stress that is causing her to forget, and therefore I can punish her if need be. For example, I keep my jeans on my side of the bedroom when I take them off because I only have two pair and wear them almost daily. If I threw them in the laundry basket each day then I would run short. She is to gather my dirty clothes up that are on my side of the bed when she does laundry each week. So, I am putting a note above the laundry basket to remind her, "Don't forget my clothes by my side of the bed." I also have a specific way of hanging my clothes in the closet (part of my OCD), so I will be hanging a note just inside the closet with a reminder on how they should be hung. With the notes posted, there should be no more "I forgot."

It's a team effort to learn to cope with problems. Instead of looking at the *dis* in disability, look at the *ability*—what *can* you do? Try to see it as a roadblock, and decide that you just have to find the way around it. Find the activities within and around that roadblock that add the individuality to your relationship.

Surrender
slave rachel

My relationship with my Master has been a roller coaster. When we first met, I was a rabid feminist, but for some reason I totally submitted to Him, not even realizing I was doing it at first. He chose my friends, my bedtime, what we did, and what happened to the money. I had a five-dollar-a-month allowance. This caused some problems, because I was often anxious about doing this when it went against my "I Am A Rock" (think Simon and Garfunkel) self-image and all of my politics and spiritual leanings. Growing up, our physician and church ministers were all women, so I only knew female authorities as final authorities. My dad taught me to cast a fishing pole accurately, to shoot guns, use bows and arrows, climb trees, hike, and fight. Most of my neighbors were boys and I was a formidable fighter and pirate, and a wannabe biker. I was supposed to grow up and be a surgeon or other physician, a minister, a poet, an artist, an astrophysicist, or a lawyer. Preferably President of the US. Certainly never a housewife or slave.

However, I think that I'm just a submissive at heart and no amount of upbringing would have changed that. Throughout high school, I had what amounted to a non-sexual M/s relationship with a friend. It was so emotionally intense that my parents tried to intervene several times. I even ran away once over it, and I gave her my heirloom ring from my great-grandmother because she admired it; she hadn't even asked for it. I spent all day at school with her, went to her house after school, and spent every weekend with her. If we were separated for a day or so, I would cry when I heard her voice again. I obeyed her completely and waited on her hand and foot. I won't go into the details, but it was pretty limitless; I would walk hours to be near her even if I only got to spend an hour with her. After I turned 18, I moved in with her. I was living with her until I met Master Richard, who immediately started limiting our contact. Eventually He forbade contact with her, as she was a bit of a threat to our relationship.

He was raised as a Jehovah's Witness by his widowed mother. This meant: No masturbation. Missionary position sex only, no foreplay. Never listen to anyone else. Do not tolerate disagreement of any kind—leave or shun them if they disagree. This still is a problem at times. He also is very socially awkward, as they do not encourage socializing except to convert or encourage each other in the service. No small talk or normal conversations. His mother was timid and passive and told her kids that being passive was more spiritual than being dominant or aggressive. This caused problems for Him, as He is naturally dominant and does it automatically. He has felt guilty over that sometimes but often doesn't realize when He is doing it. He takes over a room easily. He got elected to leadership positions in school clubs, which caused issues with his religion, and His mother made him quit the clubs.

Which brings me to the issue of dominance and submission. One thing that I have learned about natural Dominants versus acquired dominating behavior was from doing it myself. When I was doing it, I affected an angry look, staring down at people and scowling, moving quickly and aggressively as if I was going to bowl someone over, always combat-ready. It was stressful and anxiety-provoking. Natural Dominants, though, they just do it without having to affect anything. They just are. Having to be in charge can be tiring, but being a Dominant person itself is comfortable. I know at least one woman who was a natural Dominant, but she felt that it was wrong to be that way. She refused to exercise, telling me that it encouraged her to act dominant. She was actually fairly annoying, because she acted an egalitarian role, but was continually trying to take charge all the time. She ended up being perceived as self-deluded and manipulative, because she was misplacing herself. When we aren't who we are because we think it is wrong, it is often noticed as a form of fraud, even if we don't mean it that way. I know that I have been seen that way by true Dominants when I was still role playing. For me, being submissive is my nature, and in the end I found that I could not go against it.

Anyway, there was a lot of adjusting when we met. He was deeply depressed at that time. His ex had left him for another man; she was also a Jehovah's Witness, and she got the church to shun Him even though she was the "sinner" because her father was an official of the church. It was His first experience with corruption, I guess. I later found out that suicide runs rampant in his family; very deep, dark depression is common with them. (In the 1970's, depression was not thought to be chemical or biological at all.) He also had a messianic complex, which He acquired through too much dropping of acid. I would take acid and get one too, but as I came down it would go away. His didn't. So after a time, I realized he was making really bad decisions, like trading in a new car we were still making payments on for an old truck where the four-wheel-drive didn't work, or buying fifty-dollar broken cars every month.

Some guy gave Him PCP, and He thought it was just stronger pot and had a psychotic break afterwards. He ended up in hospitals, and I would go get Him out. I kept thinking that He would get over it, and bipolar was not even a word back then. His moods shifted around along with His belief systems. I learned to pay the bills, get a job, go to school, and get a better paying job. If our bills didn't need to be paid with my income, and I still needed to work some, I would do a more menial service job. I was always happier in those. Of course, when people have jobs, they make friends with co-workers, and my co-workers would tell me that I should be spending the money on myself and doing what I wanted, so I decided I needed to really take over. His constant shifting around mentally and not paying bills He didn't like convinced me that was needed.

So I became the Dominant. He and I fought a lot over it, but I became more adept at winning, and He then got a couple of concussions that created brain damage and made Him even impulsive, rage-a-holic, emotionally labile etc. So I took over even more. Basically, He lost my confidence in His abilities ... and *He* lost His confidence in *His* abilities. For about a decade and a half I was the decision-maker. This was necessary to some degree, but it became a habit even as He began to recover with no more hard drugs and no more concussions. I began to develop contempt for Him as He slowly developed into a whiny, passive-aggressive person who was manipulative and sneaky about things. I would decide that we were going somewhere and I would ask him where He wanted to go. He would say "What difference does it make? We go wherever you want anyway." I would persist, and He would finally tell me. We always went where He said, and in reality we rarely went where I wanted to go with this game, but He would not own it.

This added to my contempt, because I hate manipulation, and not owning your desires and needs, and whining. I became very disrespectful verbally and in my behavior. I no longer asked His opinion about buying things like cars; I just did it, and if He didn't like it, tough. I was sarcastic and made it clear that I was *never* getting emotionally or romantically involved again with anyone. (I didn't know that it was not just the situation but the unnatural Dominance that was getting to me.) He got used to it and got lazy. He was pissed that I was making the decisions, but also got used to not being responsible about anything. He would not get a job (probably couldn't keep one anyway with the bipolar), though for almost a year He had a store; He wouldn't help with housework even though I was working full time, going to school, and raising kids. Sometimes he would do a few dishes or make dinner— usually macaroni and cheese. He did as little as possible. Mostly He just hung out and played on the internet, smoked pot, and napped. This also added to my contempt. Every therapist I went to in order to get tips on how to handle the situation told me to leave. I didn't. Why? I guess my internal slavery explains it, because it defies logic.

At the time I was still in major denial of my slave orientation, because I believed that it was not a good thing to be that way. I even believed that these things happened in part to help me get out of that orientation and become the Dominant I thought I ought to be. Being a slave was scary and dangerous, and probably a mental defect. Still, when push came to shove, if He got assertive or took control, I would listen and do what He said. Otherwise I did what I thought we should do.

Eventually I couldn't do it anymore. I needed to be a slave, and I talked to enough other slaves to realize that it is OK to be that way. Once I began to give power back to Him, He began to slip back into His Dominant personality, though He is now more concerned about doing it "right", because he knows I can take it back, or leave, if necessary. This has changed some things, obviously. I cannot not be His slave if I am still carrying around contempt for Him; if He is going to be the Master, first I had to see *my* place. I had to let go and hand back control. I had to explore my feelings and why they were there. This meant reliving them, warts and all. So I first worked at curtailing my negative attitudes and thoughts, my reactions of sarcasm, etc..

He tested me a little to see if I was serious and really going to become obedient again, and it really added to His confidence when I followed through. It also helped that He had become more successful with His decisions. His brain has healed a lot, and only once in a while—once a month or less—does He have a really bad day.

It is difficult because when He is "off". He is not realistic. He gets extreme and wants me to change according to His belief *du jour*. Being bipolar, He can switch back in a day or two, and his new beliefs can be opposite what he believed the previous day, and if I disagree, He will not speak to me. He often threatens to leave if I do not accept His current idea when He is in His broken-brain mode. This used to scare me, and I did quietly figure out finances for both of us in case He did it. When He is like this, He gets paranoid and accusatory about anything. For example, if we were traveling and I miss an off-ramp, He will rage that I did it on purpose just to control the trip, which is absurd. When He is better, He will recognize his error and apologize.

Some days He is an atheist, other days He believes in God. I just wait it out and try to keep occupied. I don't take it seriously or personally, and I remember that it is a malfunction that rights itself. Sometimes He has threatened to release me on those days, which is scary, but I did tell Him after a few times that if He released me that I would find another Master. He doesn't want that, and when He is feeling good (which is most of the time), He likes being the Master.

Today, as I write this, is actually one of *those* days. We were talking about love, and He was saying that the Jehovah's Witnesses don't teach love at all and don't love anyone at all. I told him that I thought they taught to love within limits, and they let themselves feel a certain amount, and then withdraw or suppress it if the person "fails the organization", that they can't let themselves love freely, but they don't reject love entirely. His stand today is that there is either unconditional love or nothing, and that anything else is varying degrees of hate. He is telling me that they (and we) hate people less or more, not love them less or more. (He is in "glass half empty" mode right now.) So right now He is downstairs "trying to deal with your views about your strange idea of love."

Now He has called to let me know He is meditating and still loves me.

So I remind myself of the best part of His abilities, stay out of His way, and wait it out. I do what I can to keep occupied, be helpful, and not irritate Him. These times do tend to shake His confidence in Himself again. He is often oblivious to what is going on while it is happening—it is almost like a seizure, as His appearance somehow changes as well, and anti-seizure medication does sometimes control it, so it could well be a form of seizure. It can resolve in seconds or days.

The episodes shake my confidence a little too, but I know that they will pass. I know when He is good, He is good. So I hang on to that. I keep those memories alive on the bad days. I do think I go into survival mode when He gets that way. When He gets over it, I do get a bit of a post-traumatic thing, but I try to recognize it, process it and move on rather than act on it.

Right now I am just staying out of His way. I will get the bills paid, maybe clean up the bathroom, get His favorite pizza, and hope it passes soon.

So I've gone from obedience to reeling to Dominance to contempt to authenticity, which necessitated a radical change from the way things had become, and in some ways is a return to the beginning, with new information. I have been able to redevelop some respect for Him, and some trust. Apparently I just do not respect people I can dominate, and cannot respect a partner who doesn't dominate me.

If you are a submissive in a relationship with a Master who develops something like this, remember that it is not your fault, and that you can't fix it. Know that you *may* have to take control at times, but try not to get into that mode as a way of thinking. Remember that you *are* a slave, and it is OK to be one, and that you *can* serve by controlling a situation ... to a point. Have your Master's back, but don't try to control your Master. Understanding when your taking over the situation isn't needed at the moment, and don't get used to being dominant all the time. Sometimes you need to get out of the way, because you cannot have a rational conversation with irrational people. Sometimes a lot of emotional detachment is needed. Keep busy and try not to get too anxious.

Communicate when communication is doable. For example, He would rage at me before I went to work because He'd had a bad dream about me doing something. I would go to work all stressed out, thinking of what to do and how to cope, maybe making plans to separate in case He had decided to break up with me by the time I got home from work. I wouldn't hear from Him all day and tension would build; calling home often led to more attacks, so I learned not to "test" the waters, but to wait. So after a day of stress, I would get home and He would be over it—sitting there happy and playing with his camera or something. He would be oblivious to all of the stress He had caused me.

However, right then was *not* the best time to talk about it, as it was too fresh for me. Neither was it useful to do it during an episode. I learned to wait, and when He was in a good frame of mind the next day, I would gently tell Him that when He is angry with me in the morning but then feels better later, to *please* call and let me know so I won't stress all day for nothing. He does this now. He has told me that my standing order is to never give in when He is like this. I am to remain defiant and trust that He will recognize the need later.

You need to get very good at forgiveness, as they will often say many mean things if they want to drag you into their mood with them. Misery does love company. When they are agitated, *we* need reassurance too, but they are unable to give it. Remember that it is not on purpose. We slaves have to be calm and move forward in what we need to do that day. Trying to cajole or elicit reassurance often gets the opposite at those moments.

It helps to work a lot on what being a slave means, and how you can adapt your slavery to the situation. You need to learn to keep your focus and not get confused in what you are doing, and then get frustrated because you are controlling more than you need to. If you are actually oriented to be a natural slave, that helps because the ways come more instinctively, and feeling alive and at home in it makes it more of a non-struggle to maintain ... but feeling obligated to keep doing more to fix things (which you can't do) can lead to inappropriate controlling (even if it is well-meant) and can muddy where submission ends and where overkill begins. That is why it is important to approach your Master as a slave and consider how best to *serve*, not cure— to *protect*, not rescue—which I found, once I accepted myself, that I could do. Before, I was fighting it (both slavery and Him) and I thought that I should fight it. That was the wrong way to handle it.

If your Master has mental problems ... well, be sure that He has at least some integrity, is a good human being, and is inherently physically safe, and then you can maintain some trust in the foundation. If the Master is given to dishonesty or evasion, insecure mind games (beyond the mental illness). or physical abuse, it will be next to impossible if not impossible to maintain trust.

Trying to *give* reassurance to your Master can also be problematic, as it can open a whole new can of worms. Sometimes a kind word is good, but not too many, as you might give them enough rope to hang yourself with and give them more ammunition. It is very tempting to "smooth it over" and then re-approach the issue right away to get our own reassurance and comfort, and end up just getting into hot water again. They can't do it when they are in crazy mode. It's better to wait.

So I just tell Him I love Him and drop it.

I have learned that He still loves me, even through the broken brain. If He releases me, He releases me (this would likely include divorce or separation)—I have figured out what to do. Then I put that aside as a tool, not a plan.

If a slave is very needy, getting involved with a very depressed or bipolar person is probably not a good idea. If He breaks up with me, I won't do it again even though I am not a needy type. At 58, I don't want to go through this again. We have spent many years waiting for his illness to pass, and we haven't entertained in about 25 years because of His moods. Overcoming depressive states, not to mention religious conditioning, takes years or even decades. That is another thing I will avoid—no fundamentalist refugees. I had no idea of the depth of confusion and control those churches have, even when a person has been gone from the church for half a century. Mental balance and religious baggage would be something I will screen for! Still, even in saying that, I am committed to Him and love Him. We will be together until He releases me, or one of us goes into the grave.

WOUNDED WARRIORS: TRAUMA

Mastering PTSD

Renee

My Master is a retired Marine who served in Vietnam as a sniper. He was a recon guy, and he was injured and sent home. He has a scar that leads from mid-chest to his groin. That's not the only scar he brought home, though. He came home with PTSD.

When we met more than 18 years ago, he started to tell me stories about his time in the service. Most of his stories were about funny pranks the men played on each other or about the women he fucked all over the world. I was in awe of how fascinating his life was but I didn't really understand at all. He was telling me only good things because he hated facing and talking about the bad things, and there were a lot of bad things.

I noticed that he watched a lot of war documentaries, so for our first Christmas together I bought a series about Vietnam from our local public television station during one of their auctions. I thought it was the perfect gift. He'd never told me that he can't watch anything about Nam, and I hadn't noticed that we were only watching documentaries about WWII.

When I gave it to him, I was so excited and proud of myself for finding the perfect gift and excited that it was our first full night together, I wanted to play it for him right away and he was so caught up in watching me be all excited he allowed it and said nothing. He didn't want to hurt me so he watched it with me.

When we went to bed that night, I was so relaxed in his arms I fell asleep rather fast. I woke when I felt the bed shaking. At first it was rather mild but was building fast until his whole body was shaking. As it became what I can only describe as "severe", I got scared. I thought he was having some kind of seizure or something. Just as I started to sit up, he let out a loud yelp and jumped up.

He started pacing and forth then threw himself on the ground and started crawling (like a sniper would). It was then I remembered my aunt telling me about her husband and what they went through when he returned from Vietnam. So I stayed very still, realizing that in his state he might not know me. He was thousands of miles away.

When he came around, he came back to bed and we talked about it. He told me that it didn't happen very often but watching anything about Vietnam seemed to trigger it. I put the videos away and stopped asking him to tell me his stories for a while.

After that I watched him and realized that if I could change the subject when it came around, I could stop him from "going there". So I figured I could stop the night issues as well. I started sleeping with my body pressed against his. That way I could feel him when he first started to shake. When I felt it, I'd kind of bump my butt into him until it stirred him awake. He'd get up and go take a shower and come back to bed. It worked. He didn't go full blast with a flashback until his body was shaking violently.

After that, I started asking him to tell me his stories again. Slowly I asked him questions about the stuff that wasn't so fun. It took a few years to get him to open up about a lot of it but over time it became easier for him. Then we started watching movies, and he'd tell me all the mistakes they made about what really happened. I'd make sure I was good and pressed up against him on those nights, and over time it became less and less necessary for me to sleep with one eye open.

Now, flashbacks are very rare. It's easier for him to talk about. He can even watch movies and documentaries now, although I try to distract him when I see his face getting too serious when he's watching them.

It's taken a lot of time for us to work through his PSTD but for the most part it's under control. It's actually one of the few things in our relationship I do have some kind of control over it, but it pleases him that I do, so it's OK.

I don't believe in avoiding triggers. I think you have to face them and find a way to deal with them. It makes life easier in the long run.

Interview with Brian

Brian (with help from his slave pais)

Tell us about yourself and your relationship.

pais:

We've been together over seven years, and been M/s for six and a half. It is a no-limits relationship. 24/7, and has been since it started. That's the short summary. Originally I was looking for a female sub, because my dominant of the time was uncomfortable with me playing with anyone other than a female sub.

Brian:

I was looking for a summer fling. I was about to move to Florida, and I didn't want to, and I was looking for anything that would make me feel better at that point. I only wanted a fuck buddy, so there was no reason for her partner to feel threatened.

pais:

So we both went into it thinking it was going to be a short term … you know, no strings attached. But within two months it was clear things were heading in a different direction.

Tell me about Brian's issues.

Brian:

It's largely trauma-based. I had early childhood abuse and neglect. My mother went into a very crazy place, apparently due to 1970's medications for hysterectomies. We had some issues there with emotional abuse—locking me in the basement for the day, things like that. Later, when I had my slave pais, some of the issues that came to a sticking point for us were things like when my mother would start to go off the deep-end, she would withdraw first and become very inaccessible, so that sends me into a bit of a panic. Before she would go completely nuts, she would shut down, then flip and go berserk. So that was super triggering for me, and that's something we've had to work through.

pais:

This was a problem because I shut down when things go badly. When I get upset, nobody's home.

Brian:

So part of my coping mechanisms for the abuse—such as being locked in the basement—was to develop a fairly detailed kind of ... well, not a full-fledged alternate personality, but as pais puts it, "features of DID". Actually, I think they're bugs, not features, but it's similar in many ways to DID. I've had periods of time loss and dissociation when pushed to extreme places where the alternate personality has taken over. I did a lot of repression and strict maintenance of my feelings, and in any kind of intense emotional situation I would just shut down, for years if necessary.

Part of our early relationship was fighting through all of the guilt and shame around wanting to hurt people. That was deeply tied into that feeling of, "I have this thing inside, and if I let it out, I'm going to kill somebody. I'm going to go berserk, I'm going to lose time, and I'm going to come back covered in blood, and I'm not going to know what's happened." That was my whole life from sixth grade on. As soon as I started feeling any negative emotion I would just clamp down on it. "Can't do that."

pais:

Really early on—right around the time he collared me—I knew he was holding something back, and I basically said to him, "If you trust me, you'll let me see that, and if you can't share that with me then you don't trust me, and if you don't trust me how can I trust you?" So ... I met his alter—we call him Kevin—and I fell in love with Kevin. You might think of it as kind of a poly relationship, but with only two bodies. It was always very clear that Kevin was not my owner. Brian is my owner, and Kevin is just ... there. Brian's in control of Kevin to a very high degree, except in certain circumstances where we're very clear that he is being let out. Kevin is scary, but then also I'm a masochist, so it all worked out.

Then he started work on integrating himself. So now there's much less of him having discrete separate personalities, like alters. That was actually kind of sad for me at certain times, even though I knew it was healthy and good for him. There were moments where it got confusing because some of Kevin's traits would show up, but it wasn't actually Kevin any more. Before, I had it down, I knew how it was structured, and then it changed. For the first couple of years it was very clear, and then as he started doing the work to integrate there were some scary moments. He had times of saying, "Is this the right way to go? Should I even let myself be a whole person?" But all through it he was totally functional. I mean, he had clearly had some problems in his life, but overall he was a functioning human adult.

Brian:

The M/s definitely helped to heal me. Some of that healing is specific to the relationship between the two of us and not M/s, per se, before we were even M/s. First I had to deal with my suppressed memories. I had blocked out most of the childhood abuse, and I didn't know why I had this going on in my head. It was very confusing, and it took having somebody that I truly felt loved the parts of me that I didn't love to do that. I needed to look at it through her eyes and see that there was some value there to those parts, too. That started to unlock all the locks and doors and tripwires and booby-traps that I had placed around the pit that Kevin was in. I started to engage, and I finally felt safe enough to have essentially what was a very brief nervous breakdown, and I started digging up little bits here and there until finally the story got very clear. But I don't think I could have done that on my own. I wouldn't have had the incentive to do it. There would have been no one to do it for. I was fairly functional, and if I was experiencing negative emotions, well, who does that hurt, aside from me? That's the way I was looking at it.

Where the M/s comes into play has been in how I handled the integration. I needed to feel that if in the process of starting to feel anger again, I got really blindingly upset about something and did something stupid, I'm doing it to somebody I own who will probably get off on it anyway. But I didn't believe it at first! That's why it took two years. I didn't believe that it would be OK; I didn't believe that any part of feeling anger or upset was going to be worthwhile.

pais:

But see, that's ridiculous because DID usually takes a long time to fix. You're usually in therapy for thirty years with that. People don't usually get all better in just a couple of years. It's all right to be still working on it.

Brian:

Fortunately I don't have severe DID. I wasn't flipping out randomly at work. What I had was relatively minor, for which I'm infinitely grateful because it's scary when that happens. I feel like I've been carefully defusing a bomb for a few years, but... more for me than for her, and I think that what makes it safe for her is that we now have a deeper relationship—a more honest and fully fledged human relationship where everybody feels all their own emotions and doesn't have to shove anything down. That's also why I'm so particular about making sure she shows me what she's feeling, because I know what comes from cramming all that stuff down, and it's not good. But I don't actually feel like she was unsafe at any point.

We don't use a punishment context, and while part of that is because it was bad for her, part of it was also that it didn't work well for me. We did corporal punishment once or twice in the beginning, and then we tried to play and she flinched, and that was done forever. It definitely pushed a lot of my "You flinched, I'm not safe," buttons. A big part of why I could open up to her in the first place was because she wasn't afraid of me. There was nothing in me that she was afraid of, no matter how vile, or sadistic, or ridiculous, or terrible. I wouldn't generally suggest waiting for somebody else to love you before you can love yourself, but it helps.

pais:

Yeah, that's kind of like the opposite of what people should do. For some people it may be the only way there, but I don't want to make it sound like, "Oh, sure, there's mental illness, but if somebody loves you, everything will be fine."

So pais trusts you. How do you trust yourself?

Brian:

When I came to this relationship, it had been ten years since I felt like I had a loss of control over my behavior. I'd been pushed very hard by a relationship with someone who had bipolar, and I survived that without going off. So I felt that if I could get through that, then I had it enough under control to be responsible. Plus I'd already had two children, so I'd been responsible for someone else's life for a good eight years by the time we got together. I don't know that there's a good benchmark; there's no set of years or miles that's going to help you with your warranty.

Being in a relationship with my former partner's mental health issues didn't help. It was certainly making things worse, because I had to bottle up all my problems, and the more I bottled them up, the more of them there were! It felt like a time bomb, which is why I ended the relationship. I felt like it wasn't good for either of us. In contrast, I had a good basis of understanding with pais about how the situation might unfold. I owned the fact that I might get violent if something very triggering happened, but the things the trigger me are very far from the places where we go together. For example, there's a possibility that I might get triggered by sudden unexpected physical violence, but that is not something I'm ever going to expect from pais. She's never someone who lashes out physically. I've been in relationships with people who did, and I learned that I could take it—if they're going to freak out, and I'm going to come home and unexpectedly get hit, I can take it. But I don't want to push that possibility any more.

I don't know if there's any good benchmark for how safe (or not) you are if you have particularly violent urges. I think that it's important that the other person knows about it and knows what can trigger it, and that you both dig deep into everything you can think of that can set it off, but ideally you should get together with somebody who doesn't want to do those triggering things. There are people who like to push those buttons, especially people who grew up with domestic violence, abusive situations, or domestic violence situations. That's a bad mix. The downside of my "white knight syndrome" was finding a lot of people who were in a bad situation and wanted somebody to Dom them into a good relationship or out of a bad one.

That wasn't pais, although she does have her own childhood abuse issues going on. I think, in many ways, she'd be perfectly happy if I would lash out at her—for example, if the way I expressed my displeasure was to get in her face and make her feel small and scared, some part of her would welcome that, as that's how people expressed their displeasure in her early world. That's what she grew up with during her entire childhood. I figured it out early on—she certainly didn't needle me about it, but she kept expressing, "It would be all right if you did! It's OK! I don't mind!" It was more of a helpful suggestion: "If you're someone who has bottled-up anger issues, you can just take them out on me! I don't mind!" But it became clear that it was not a healthy thing for her, so I wouldn't do it.

Have you ever tried to see a kink-aware therapist about any of this?

Brian:

I never even tried, to be honest. It's so far out of my comfort zone in a lot of different ways. I haven't had good experiences with medical professionals in general, and I'm all too aware of the human frailties that get in the way. It's good that it's an option, and it's definitely something that I would do if I felt that I was unsafe, or that it was impacting my ability to work or maintain my relationships, or in any way risked my kids. I've had some bad times, but not for any prolonged length of time. Besides, the only kink-aware person I know of who does M/s relationship therapy in this area is seeing a lot of other people that I know, which makes me pretty uncomfortable. I feel like they're the therapist for the entire community, and that's weird. There aren't enough M/s-aware options out there. Therapy's good, but maybe you can do it yourself if you have the tools. I was blessed with a highly introspective step-father who gave me a lot of tools for how to deal with things. If it had only been my father teaching me, I would have been kept it bottled up for the rest of my life.

What advice would you give for an s-type who's looking at a dominant who just told them, "Hi, I have this history of abuse, and it's messed with my head in certain ways, and I've got triggers and I've got baggage," etc.

pais:

You need to look at the whole picture, because how an abuse history manifests with one person is going to be totally different from how it might present from somebody else. And please go slow! Get to know someone well; don't give away your whole life the day that you meet someone, or even two months after you've met them. It takes time to really get to know someone. And don't try to fix them! No "white knights" on the bottom side either. You couldn't, even if you had the power in the relationship.

Also, know yourself and what level of uncertainty you're willing to live with. I think that s-types really crave a certain amount of predictability. Now sometimes mental illness can look very predictable—I know exactly what some of his triggers are, and I know exactly what it's going to look like if he gets triggered. Once I had that information, it was all good. But other kinds of mental illness can be very unpredictable, so know what you can live with.

But if you've got somebody who has the insight to come to you and say, "Look, I have this history and here's what happens," I would say that's a fantastic sign that this is someone who's done a lot of work, who's really in touch with what's going on, and probably has a fairly good handle on it. I would be much more concerned about the Dom who doesn't tell you, who says that everything is fine and that they have no problems. Especially when it's clear that something serious is going on, but even when it's not— everyone is a human being, and everyone has their own little quirks.

Brian:

Taking it slow is good. Keep in mind that things can be really unpredictable, so I would suggest that you both try to find coping strategies that will give the s-type some kind of agency to deal with it if the dominant gets badly triggered. For example, if two years down the road they are suddenly laid off from their job, stress levels in the house go through the roof, behaviors you've never seen before are crawling out, and you've already given yourself over to their judgment. Think about that situation, and talk to the dominant about it. What could you do to help them through that part? Or, if the two of you agree it's not a situation that would be safe for you, how do you extract yourself from it in a meaningful way? Really think it through, if it's a dangerous situation.

pais:

We had that conversation and we decided that I would just go crazy, too, if that happened, and that we'd both just be crazy together.

Brian:

But it's important to have the conversation, to at least make sure that everyone understands what the possibilities are. The dominant should ask themselves honest questions too. How do you feel you would react in this situation where you are under ten thousand times the stress of a normal day? Or, for instance, I think you've cheated on me? What are you going to do if that's a trigger of yours? How's that going to make you feel? Are you going to fly off the handle? The more forthright someone can be about their issues, the safer I would feel. If they can talk about it, and not just in a vague, theoretical kind of way, but in a real, heartfelt way, if it's more important to them that you be safe than that they feel "domly" ... I think that's the touchstone I would look for. What's the priority? Is the priority, like, the fetishy, ego-based "I'm completely in charge of myself," or is it the reality-based, "Are we actually taking care of real people here, and seeing them as actual people?"

There's a lot of denial in the M/s demographic about masters having baggage and triggers and other difficult things. Many of them pretend that nothing's wrong, or they are afraid to talk about it for fear of being judged inadequate as a master. There's more leeway for s-types to have problems, for reasons that are rather insulting to s-types, but mostly around "At least they're not the ones with power in the relationship!" How do you feel about that, and how do you think we can change that?

Brian:

I think we're getting a good start on it at live support groups and sometimes at the Master/slave Conference. The masters come out and talk about it in person, face-to-face, in a place where it's not stored digitally forever. But we need the online forums to be places where masters can feel comfortable speaking up about these things. We also need books like this and just getting it out there. I've been in a lot of demographics and communities, both fringe and mainstream, and everybody everywhere's got baggage. The competent CEO has baggage. Even the president has shit, and that doesn't make them incompetent in doing their job. I think the cause is partly the stigma of having baggage, as if that was the worst thing that you could possibly do. Part of it is the general dehumanization in our society around people having any kind of negative histories or triggers, and part of it is the stereotype about dominants being crazy people who want to cut your arm off.

The best thing we could do is try to address these issues. Masters and slaves are just people. They're people who are comfortable in these relationships, and the Great Unspoken Secret is that many of us are in these relationships because it helps us with those issues. We feel safer, either because we feel like we'll be able to control the situation and not get our triggers pushed, or because we need to feel not in control, because being in control of the situation pushes our triggers. And that's OK. It's really OK. If you're in a relationship that's functioning well for you, and it's not making things worse, it's actually making them better, then it's great. It's no different than finding that you're happiest in any other kind of relationship, for any reason at all.

Interview with Ki
Ki (with help from her slave Bella)

(Note: Ki has DID—Dissociative Identity Disorder, formerly known as Multiple Personality Disorder, so she is using the self-referential plural pronouns "we" to indicate all the "alters" in her "system". Bella also sometimes refers to Ki as "they" in this interview for the same reason.)

Ki:

I'm Ki, and a lot of other people too. I'm also the master of my slave Bella. We are diagnosed with multi-origin PTSD, caused by being raped incestuously and also raped outside the family line. We are diagnosed with Bipolar Type 1, rapid-cycling, rage tandem. We are diagnosed with Dissociative Identity Disorder; we stopped counting at a hundred and fifty people in here. Counting became irrelevant at that point. We are a co-conscious shattered system—co-conscious because we do have one person in here who is in charge of the damn library, so that when Jessica leaves the keys God only knows where, someone can look and say, "Where are they?" When I couldn't find my keys in my pouch this morning, it was Eric who said, "Look in the pocket of the jeans you're wearing." Jeans? Right. I hadn't put them on, I didn't know I was wearing them. Most systems have a bunch of whole people with a few cracks through them. Ours is like a plate-glass window that's been dropped. You've got some big parts, some tiny little slivers of personality, and everything in between. That's a shattered system.

We are also anthropophobic. Technically that means that we are afraid of people, but we're afraid of people because we are afraid for people. We are in a large body with four unarmed combat training styles under our belt. Martial arts, military style, law enforcement, and street-fighting because we were in juvenile hall for some time, under a protection program because we testified against our rapist. You put all those unarmed combat styles in the same body with a rage disorder, and then piss us off? Put us in a WalMart with the stupid people? We don't want to harm anybody, so we're not afraid of them, we're afraid for them, and we do everything we can to keep ourselves separated. The only reason we can function in a BDSM venue is because there is a very strict set of rules. People don't try to come up and hug you without warning.

So those are our four diagnoses, mentally. We have been in therapy since 1985, treating the rape PTSD. In 1991, we bounced our nine-month-old daughter off a bed, and almost bounced her off a cinder brick wall. At that point, we packed her and our three-year-old son up, took them to juvenile, and said, "Keep them safe ... and get me some fucking help, because that is not what a mother is supposed to want to do. There's something wrong here." It took them four more years to find the bipolar. Once they found it, they tried treating it with talk therapy, group therapy, and medication. We found out that we were allergic to a number of the medications, starting with Lithium. We got far too friendly with walls, furniture, floors, and doors; we couldn't walk at all. It took a number of years before we found the right cocktail. If we do not take our medication for about three days, we get screwed up and it's going to take us a week to get back on track. We are still in talk therapy to this day, and we have built up a very large support group of people that we can openly talk to. We had to train our therapist about the BDSM and the M/s—do some diversity training and explain how it works. After that, it was all good.

So the big ugly uncomfortable thing being said among M/s people is that if you have so many things that might knock you out of control, how can you possibly be in control of someone else? How do both of you deal with that?

Bella:

First, I knew about everything going into it. I didn't take her collar and then six months later get told, "Oh, by the way, I have all these issues, but I didn't want to mention them." They were very up-front about their problems and what might happen. There are times when they will stay in bed with bipolar chemical issues for two or three days, getting up only to eat, and I'm not supposed to talk to them. The main reason this works is because my tagline is, "Own your shit". They do their best to own everything that happens. If they notice that they are getting cranky, or getting depressed, they communicate that. I weighed it all out in the beginning, because I'd just gotten out of a power dynamic relationship with someone who was undiagnosed bipolar and resisted treatment, and the rage had been escalating over the years. Even though it was supposed to be a power dynamic with me on the right side of the slash, I had all the responsibility for doing everything. It was all kinds of wonky.

Ki:

That relationship had ended up being physically and mentally abusive, and it made her very wary.

Bella:

So when we entered this one, for the first year we very tentatively tested everything. "Can I cope with this? Will it affect my children? Will this be too awful?" I tested all of that before I agreed to anything major. To this day, if they're having a particularly bad day or week, I will reassess if this is still healthy for both of us—and if it's not, is it fixable? Is there something we can work on? That keeps getting assessed every single time.

Ki:

From both sides! As an example, we were sleeping two hours out of every forty-eight, and then maybe ten hours, and then two hours out of the next forty-eight. And that does something to a mood—whatever's wrong, sleep deprivation makes it worse. It takes me right down. She was frustrated, because we did want to get back on a schedule, so we'd tell her to go ahead and wake us up. She'd try to get us up at ten in the morning when we hadn't fallen asleep until six—or seven, or eight—and we wouldn't wake up, we'd tell her to come back later. She'd get frustrated with that—"You told me to wake you up, and you aren't waking up!" So she put that in her journal that I read—"I'm frustrated, damn it, own your shit! I can't do this without you!" OK, that means something is really wrong. And something was—it turned out that we were missing one of the medications that regulates our sleep. So she looks at us, and tells us when we're off. When we see those signs, we have to do something about it.

Since there's a whole lot in your life that's out of control, or at least not perfectly under control, does being entirely in control of one other person, as much as you can be, does that help?

Ki:

Having a slave gives us a reason to be in control of ourselves. We can hold it together for her, and for our House, our capital-H organization—because we will not dishonor ourselves, we will not dishonor her, we will not dishonor our House. We will not be less than appropriate, regardless of how frustrating that A-word is. We guide ourselves by that. We've been in therapy for decades, and we have learned everything we have been able to find about our challenges. I don't say "illnesses", because DID is not an illness; it's a unique coping skill. The problem with it is that once you use it as a coping skill, it becomes your best coping skill, so as soon as there is another challenge, you make another person, because that's the coping skill you've learned. But the other three are definitely illnesses.

To be a master with a mental illness, you have to have a tighter rein on yourself and an exceptional amount of self-awareness. With every new therapist we get, we get three comments: "You're highly intelligent, you're highly creative, and you have an amazing amount of self-awareness." Because without those, it ain't gonna happen. You've got to be bright enough to solve problems, you've got to be creative enough to work around things, and you've got to be self-aware enough to spot your issues before they affect others. On top of that, you've got to be humble enough to see them and do something about them. There is no room for ego if you're going to be a master with mental challenges. When the girl looks at me and says, "You're out of control," or "You're irrational," I have to accept that we are out of control and irrational, and we need to go find the source. That means that I put a great deal of trust in her. We have literally put our lives in her hands.

A slave is a resource. Are there ways in which you use your living resource to help yourself?

Ki:

Damn skippy! There are a number of situations where you do not tell us No. It's a trigger, because of the anthropophobia and the PTSD. As my therapist puts it, I am highly functional in a calm setting, but I decompensate quickly under stress. I just want to pick the obstacle up by the throat and bash them into a wall until they are a bloody pulp. There are times when we have had to talk ourselves down from driving our van through the front of a building because someone in it pissed us off. We have learned not to travel alone, and we usually don't even go outside the house alone; she's with us as an escort. She may put herself as a shield between us and a potential problem, or entirely head off a potential problem. My psych has written a letter saying "I don't care who you are, you don't send her in anywhere alone. There will be someone who is trained to handle her with her at all times. You send the handler with her, or you will get hurt."

The strongest example of this was when we had to have an endometrial ablation last November. We were not happy about having to do this in the first place, and now they want to put us in a hospital, put us under anesthesia, so we'll be in a twilight zone as we come out of it. Our first concern was that someone would touch us, and we were not going to have enough control due to the anesthesia, and we were going to pop somebody. They're going to see a fat housewife. They are not going to see military and martial arts training, and they are not going to expect violence. So we emphasized that she had to be with us, but when they started to take us in, they told us that she was not allowed to come. I was triggered, and I said two words: "Fix this!" After that point, it was her problem. It's taken a lot of trust to come to the point when I can let go and let it be her problem now.

We've had somebody try to take us back into a medical office for Social Security, and they said she couldn't come. A friend of ours here in the BDSM community has decided that we are able to teleport, because we can go from here to there so quickly when triggered, and that's pretty much what we did. We went right into the woman's face, because we were triggered—we were being told to go into a new situation without somebody to be that shield. When we were in the hospital, she talked with them. She made them understand that they could not have us conscious without her at our side. So when we passed out, she was there, and when we woke up, she was there. That became its own hell, and she should tell you what happened, because we weren't exactly there for that.

Bella:

I'd already talked to the anesthesiologist and they understood that when they brought her around, I should be there. They got that part, and when she came out of surgery they had us in a little isolation room. There was a nurse around, and I explained to her, "Rape victim just had surgery on girl parts! Rage, dissociative, and multiple types of combat! Just let me handle her." So she started to come to, and the first thing she did was to grab hold of the rails of the bed and apparently try to turn the whole thing over. She was trying to rock it in order to get up. I spent the next hour standing by a bed that was about chest height on me, taking hold of her hand, and arm-barring her in the chest to push her back into the bed. About the third time she woke up, I finally got some sort of consciousness and not just a physical response, so I started the "Look at me. Right here. Right here. It's OK."

When she finally came around, she said, "I gotta go." I thought she meant that she had to leave, so I told her that we couldn't go anywhere, we'd just had surgery, it's OK, I'm right here. Then I got the six-year-old in her system coming out and yelling, "I gotta go pee!" That I could handle! I talked to the nurse, who said that she could go right there and they would clean it up. But the six-year-old yelled, "I can't go right here!" so we got a bedpan under her. She scared the nurse by how high she bridged her body, even right after surgery—she has a lot of strength in her legs. When I was arm-barring her earlier, I was also making sure that she wasn't getting her legs under her, because as long as it was only the upper body I actually had a chance. If she got her legs involved, I would have been screwed. The six-year-old couldn't use the bedpan either, and I had to comfort her. Then she started developing a migraine, and I reassured her that there were meds in the IV for that.

They finally got her CPAP and I handed it to her—it's a trigger because every night she'll try to take it off, so she built in an automatic reflex to put the mask back on every time I tell her to. But if anyone else tried to put something on her face in that situation, she would freak. So she put the CPAP on herself, and the nurse looked at me like I was crazy because I wasn't doing it for her, but she did go to sleep.

Another half an hour went by, and she woke up with a cry, and I said, "You already have medication, and you're sleeping it off." Then they wanted us to leave that area and go to another area. I described this as being like wrestling a camel, because she is large and strong and has two big humps. The rage kicked in because she wanted to leave, and I had to literally get in her face and say, "OK, you want to go home? We can go home, but this is what you have to do. You have to breathe for me so that you will pass your oxygen test. You need to not clock the nurse because that will piss them off, and they will send you to the psych ward, and you need to have patience with me and trust that I will fix this." We did finally get out of there, but you have to understand that one of the first orders that I received in this power dynamic was to take care of their health. That is part of my service, and a big part of my job. To an outsider, it might have seemed like I was the caretaker, I was in control, she was helpless under me, and I was the one who was doing everything. Technically true, perhaps, but I was doing it all as a service to make sure that she would be safe and healthy, and that everything would get done properly. It did not wonk the power dynamic because I was doing it all for them, on their orders. She put her trust in me to make sure that she would be safe, the doctors would be safe, and she would not end up in the psych ward.

Ki:

And I've trained her to do all of that, to be all of that for me. I've trained her how to phrase things with doctors, how to deal with us when we're in crisis, how to come near us, how to wake us up, or when not to. When we go into a restaurant, she makes sure that our back is to a wall. Right now we get triggered when we see cars that were made between 1985 and 1995, because one of our triggers is seeing car accidents, from back when we were doing Search and

Rescue, and we saw a lot of those cars; so when we see one on the highway we get a startle reflex. We have to remind ourselves that there isn't any blood, it's not an accident to respond to, everything is OK. She's learned to talk us down from a lot of those. Some of that she had before we got hold of her; some of that was trained specifically for us. Sometimes the rage does go off at her, but the first thing out of her mouth is "Red", and then I walk away.

Bella:

The safeword always works, because they've hardwired it in so that it is beyond any other response. It is still scary for me; my ex-husband who had undiagnosed bipolar did get violent with me. Bipolar does look the same no matter who's got it—the tone of voice, the body language, the energy that comes off of it—it's all very similar, so it's very triggering for me to deal with that. But I have learned to have faith that it is not going to become what it was with him, and to know that if I safeword, they will always turn around and walk away. On the other hand, having been in this relationship for a while, I also know how not to escalate it. I don't follow them around after I've safed and insist on talking. If they are obviously giving me short, snappy responses—or completely irrational ones—I recognize that there is something bad going on. I need to not take it personally, I need to find a good time in the next few minutes to let them know about it—"Are you aware that you might be a little off today?"—so that they have a chance to check and see what's going on.

Ki:

And when we hear that, it's our responsibility to say, "OK, what's going on with us?" We need to find the source of the problem and try to fix it.

Bella:

So I work to make sure that I've got the coping skills to handle that, and if something she does is horribly triggering to me, I will own that, because she's in a place where she can't own it right now. I'll write it out in my journal and do whatever I need to do to work myself through it in that moment, and know that later—either that evening or the very next day, sometime when the chemical levels have evened out again—I will bring that up. They may have read it in the journal by that time, and we'll discuss the interaction and how we could have made it go better, or how to fix whatever got damaged if there was no way for it to go better.

Ki:

There's nobody in my system that dislikes Bella. There are some people in here who don't really care much for anybody—their job is one thing or another and they don't give a flying fahoozle about what's going on out here, they don't actively like or love her—but there's nobody that dislikes her.

What about when you're put in the position of caretaker and it's not what you would have chosen—how do you keep yourself in the dynamic while acting like this? How do you balance that?

Bella:

The balancing act usually comes later. You have to give yourself permission—and the master-person has to give you permission—to be whatever you need to be to fulfill their orders. If I'm being Mommy-like toward her, or if I'm being a dominant bitch in the doctor's office, I have the freedom to do that. It doesn't define all of me, but what I'm doing is absolute in that moment. There's no thinking about how I am a slave in the back of my mind while this dominant bitch is telling the nurse, "This is not happening!" That right there is what's real in that moment. Later on, when I'm processing, I might realize that maybe I was more dominant than her at that point, because dominance and submission is a range, not a point, and we slide back and forth along it. If you had to be dominant over here, that doesn't make you any less submissive over here later on. I can't be completely slave-like and be the dominant that my children need at the same time—that doesn't work. I just became the person I needed to be to provide that service, based on the orders I was given.

My first rule is to take care of myself, because I can't take care of anybody else if I haven't taken care of myself. Taking care of myself means allowing that dominant bitch to be there in that doctor's office. My second order is to take care of them, so I've followed both orders. Being what's needed doesn't take away from my role in this relationship.

Ki:

The slave also has to be careful that they do not enable their master. Slaves can be so devoted that they will just go further and further, and ignore all the red flags and pain that mental illness is causing them. When the illness gets the ride going, it can take not only the master but the slave as well. A slave in this situation needs to retain the right to walk away, if only for a short time, and the will to use it if they have to.

What advice would you have for would-be slaves who are looking at a master who's got issues like these, and wondering if they can trust this person? How do they tell if they can trust this person, and how do they cope?

Bella:

Well, first, if you come from an abusive background and you cannot deal with being yelled at, or with anger or other random emotions being directed at you, you need to know that—because you're not going to be able to magically handle it when it happens. It's not going to stop triggering you; it's not going to suddenly be OK. You need to own that, and really think about whether the benefits are worth the cost. Are you going to become too damaged by this to be able to cope with it? Own that and step away. Other than that, it's a matter of determining whether the person with these issues is actually owning them. Can you trust them to be responsible for their problems? If you can't, step away. There are other people and other relationships in the world. This might not be for you.

Look at how they are owning it. Are they communicative about it? What are they doing to help themselves? Are they in therapy? Are they taking necessary medications? What choices are they making about their life? Are they willing to work with you to set up rules and protocols to protect you? Can you say, "If you do this, it will affect me in this way; this is how I'm going to need to handle it later, and are you willing to work with that?" If they say, "I'm going to get pissed off and I'm going to yell and do crazy things because of what's wrong with me, but I don't mean it and you just need to deal with that," there's no way to have a resolution there. They might be owning it a little by walking away as soon as they've done the crazy stuff, but if you need help afterwards—with reconnecting, with understanding that they know what they've done—if you don't get that, if all you get is the weird behavior and then you have to handle it all on your own—that's probably not going to work for most people. I'm sure that there are some people who are amazingly solid and self-aware who could cope with that, but not most people.

It doesn't have to be a deal-breaker for a relationship, but they have to take responsibility every time for what their illness has done, and fix it as soon as possible immediately afterwards. And if it is a deal-breaker for you, that's OK. Again, not everybody can be a hospice nurse. Not every submissive can be comfortable with turning around and saying, "You just gave me an order that makes no sense, and you're being very loud and annoying right now, and perhaps you need a Zyprexa!" We do have rescue meds for when things get bad and can't be stabilized quickly enough, and I will ask if they need one if I think it would be useful. It's not exactly a safeword, but it's an outside checkpoint where I ask them to consider how they feel and what they might need. If you can't be that person for them, then you probably shouldn't be in that relationship because it's not going to work.

You have to be able to be emotionally independent in the moment when it's necessary. You need rules, protocols, and rituals to handle things in case they do go batshit crazy for a day, and it's going to take time for them to resolve things or let meds kick in. You need to be able to take that time for yourself and not just weep, "Oh my god, what am I going to do?" You both need to have things in place so that you have a function during that time, so that you're not going to fall apart if they are unavailable for a day or three, or a week. Think about how you are going to deal with that. If you're someone who needs micromanagement, who needs someone there to direct them 24/7 and is always there to be relied upon, don't do it. That's not the relationship for you, and you need to own that.

What would you say to masters who are wondering if they are safe enough to have a slave?

Ki:

We always wonder if we're safe enough. It's a constant check on ourselves. You can't just say, "This will be better in a year," or "This will be better if we just get the slave trained." If that is what you're thinking, you're going the wrong way.

I would say that there are some specific requirements for being owned by someone with a mental illness. If you're looking at a slave who is anything other than an alpha-type slave, who cannot look at you dead in the eye and say, "You need to sit down!" then that is not the primary slave for you. They need to have the balls to tell you firmly when you're going off, and you need to have the humility to do what has to be done. It's not about the dynamic at that point. It's everything about keeping you safe.

If the slave cannot accept that their second order is to watch over your health, that slave is not the slave for you. If that slave does not have enough self-esteem to handle your moods, and enough strength to come talk about it later instead of internalizing it, that is not the slave for you. If they are not communicative, they are not the slave for you. If they are not someone who can keep from taking things personally, and if they don't have a strong will, if they can't look at the doctor and say, "This is what they need," or look at their master and say, "You are out of control right now," then they are not the slave for you. And if you as the master cannot accept hearing that, or punish them later for it—in any way—it's not going to fly. It's not going to work.

What does the M/s demographic need to know about this sort of relationship?

Ki:

That basic open, honest communication is only the start of the level of communication needed to pull this off.

Bella:

There are a lot of different ways to look at "controlling one's self". When someone has a mental illness, or even just something like chronic pain, there will be times when they don't have the perfect control over themselves that one would have in a perfect world. But are they owning it? Are they doing everything they can to help themselves? What do they do after they have lost control for a moment? How do they fix it? What are they doing to maintain better control over themselves? How are they doing in the bigger picture? That's far more important in the long run. Don't judge someone based on this small piece.

Interview with Mistress Thorne and Railen

(Editor's Note: Mistress Thorne's story of abuse and PTSD is fairly graphic, and I'm told by some other PTSD sufferers that I should warn everyone in advance so as not to trigger people without warning. So here is your warning: if you can't read about severe and graphic abuse, skip from page 61 to page 68 and you'll be OK.)

How long have you two been together, and have you been M/s that whole time?

Mistress Thorne:

Six years, and yes! I was co-dominant with a gentleman in Albany, and Railen came to serve us. I found it necessary to take Railen under my protection because the dominant that I was living with at the time was sadistic, irresponsible, dishonest, and dangerous.

Railen:

When I first came to her, I had been serving a woman on the Internet, and Mistress recognized early on that this person was not being very honorable, and pointed that out to me. So when that relationship ended, it freed me up to be entirely with Mistress.

Mistress Thorne:

And from that moment on, Railen was extremely devoted and we had an unusual connection. I was monogamous with the man I was co-dominant with, so we had a very chaste relationship. I did not realize it at the time, but in his own way, Railen was courting me and giving me many opportunities to get to know him personally through books, music, conversation, and his service. He was extremely respectful and honorable. I noticed qualities in him that I'd never seen before, and he awakened within me emotions that I'd never experienced in my life. So it was a very affectionate relationship. We had quite a stable of slaves, but of all of them, Railen was outstanding and easily became alpha slave.

Railen:

Early on there was always challenges, because about a month after I met Mistress she fell from a horse and broke three ribs, screwed up her shoulder, and then a month later she slipped and fell again, and broke another rib.

Mistress Thorne:

I was also having emotional problems that were beginning to surface. I had been single for years prior to meeting this dominant, and he met my needs on an intellectual level. I liked his strength, but he was not intimidated by my strength either, so our co-dominant relationship was very satisfactory in many areas. It wasn't until we began to form a household and get a stable of slaves that I discovered that he basically used them, broke them, and left them for me to fix and take care of, which was totally unacceptable. When he ended the relationship, I needed a place to go, and Railen offered me shelter at his apartment, so I moved in with him at that point.

I've had chronic back problems for the last forty years. It necessitated essentially immobility and put all the responsibility on Railen for everything. I am disabled, and have been disabled since the year 2000, so I live on a fixed income, and Railen supports me financially, which I certainly am indebted to him for, but there was never any question about it whatsoever. The back problems lasted years; it's just in the last year that I'm able to walk better. I also gained seventy-five pounds of weight after the breakup, which made walking and breathing worse. I use a BiPap machine for breathing. I have chronic chest pain—so I need to take nitroglycerin—asthma, and episodes when I would use nebulizers and had adverse reactions, and the dominant I was living with would actually call Railen to come and take care of me.

Railen:

Something that I think has been ever-present, after we really had a committed and intimate relationship, was this peeling back the layers of an onion as Mistress has grown more comfortable and has the support that she needs. There are now opportunities for her to explore the deeper, darker parts of her psyche that have caused her so much trouble over the years.

Mistress Thorne:

I'm basically agoraphobic. Leaving the house for any reason has been very difficult until my latest breakdown. I've had the agoraphobia for thirty years. At one time it was so bad that I could not communicate with people or answer the telephone. I would have a panic attack if somebody rang the doorbell or knocked at the door, and I couldn't answer it. I had a psychotic break recently, and the medication was changed, and it's enabled me to be more mobile. During the most recent breakdown I attempted suicide twice, slicing my wrist on a bed frame and trying to slit my throat with a plastic butter-knife—all while on one-to-one supervision. I agreed to ECT treatments for the first time in my life, and they have dramatically affected my sense of well-being and depression, but have not affected the PTSD at all.

Could you tell me about your history of PTSD and where it came from, as much as you're comfortable with?

Mistress Thorne:

I was first raped by my father at the age of six. I'm the oldest of twelve children and my mother is developmentally disabled, and she basically just had one baby after another, and that's all that she did. She did not cook or clean or raise children. I raised the children; that was my responsibility. I remember, at the age of six, being called "the manager", and I enjoyed getting credit for my abilities. At the age of seven I would have to leave school at one o'clock in the afternoon to come home and watch the children so my father could leave for work, because he worked 3-11 and it took him time to get there. I can remember, at that age, some women from the church coming to help with child care duty, and I was very dissatisfied with their standards and their ability to care for the children.

I grew old very fast. My father educated me by having me read a lot of porn books. He would justify adults sexually using young children and young girls with anthropology books detailing the actions of priests, holy men, fathers or uncles in the tribe sexually training a young girl, so that when she got married she would not have problems with the husband; she would feel that the problems that she had were caused by men other than her husband, and thus insure a happier marriage.

I became fascinated with the world of BDSM in childhood. I was a voracious reader, and I learned how to read before I started school. I read a lot about BDSM and people being put in bondage, taken against their will, being abused, and being molested. I definitely think that I was trying to make some kind of sense out of what was going on with my family. I was submissive to my father and lived to please him, but at the same time I was clearly the alpha in the house, dominant over my mother and my siblings, and no one else ever challenged my authority. From the earliest age I can remember, I had zero tolerance for any misbehavior among the children, because it would trigger my mother into rages. She was extremely physically abusive until the sex started. After my father started raping me, she stopped beating me because I had his favor.

She was there the first time he raped me, watching from the doorway. She looked into my eyes as it happened. It was causing me a lot of pain, and I didn't know what my father was doing. I assumed it must be all right because it was my father, and my mother was right there and wasn't in any state of alarm, but then she walked away. I remember being in a tremendous amount of pain from the penetration, and very alarmed at the amount of blood, but I had no one to protect me or take care of me, so I had to take care of it. I felt very abandoned, and totally motherless, at that point.

Later on my father introduced me to sodomy, and that would cause me rectal bleeding that would last for days, which would throw me into a panic because there would be so much blood in the toilet. I didn't know about the anatomy and physiology, or how to stop it. My mother never made an issue of the blood on my underwear or said anything about it. The sex was always very painful, but my father also liked to masturbate me as well, and that was pleasurable, so I had this mixture of pleasure and pain from him. But it changed my whole routine, because after I got the children and my mother settled in bed, that was my time to do my homework and stay awake until my father came home, because I had to be awake and ready for him. To this day I have severe sleep difficulties. I panic as soon as it gets dark, because I start to get tired, and I know that I have to stay awake because my father's coming home. That went on for ten years.

Then a friend of my sister's was planning to run away, and I felt that was a foolish thing for him to do, and I met him in the evening while I was waiting for my father to come home. We went outside, and there was something about the night air ... it was wintertime, but I didn't have winter clothes. I could never remember, as a child, having clothes that actually kept me warm. I was outside, and I was cold, but there was something about the clear winter night sky, and the air. Suddenly I felt a euphoria that words could not adequately describe. I decided, yes, let's run away! But before then I had never thought about escape, or running away; I thought that my future would be that of a prostitute, because I wasn't suited for anything else. I didn't think or dream about college because even though I was an A student, I didn't feel that I had any future or any way to make my way through the world. I thought that the best I'd ever do would be to please men, because that's how I was trained.

So I ran away. I was picked up by a man, and he got rid of the boy I was with and held me against my will for a month until the police found me. During that time I was gang-raped and tortured and kept in closets. It was a nightmare. I had a debriefing with the police, and they were very kind, but when I met my father again, I asked him if things would continue the same as they had when I'd lived at home before. He said yes, they would, so I said, "Then I don't want to come home again."

I had an uncle who was older than my father, a teacher at City College of New York, and to get out of the house I would give him oral sex in his college office on the campus, or in the car on the parkway at the rest stops. I hated doing it, but it was worth getting out of the house once in a while for a field trip, so to speak. He offered his home as a refuge for me after I ran away, but his wife did not like me at all. His daughter acted very jealous. He promised that I could go to college. I had missed a lot of eleventh grade, but I was able to make up my time because of my grades.

I started seeing a psychiatrist who also molested me. When I told my aunt about the molestation, she ignored it, so I continued to see the psychiatrist, and it was very traumatic every time I saw him. When I refused to go, he would give me sample drugs—Quaaludes and other psychoactive drugs—not as a prescription, but just to try, like candy. I stockpiled them so that I could commit suicide, but my aunt found my stash and got rid of it, so I wasn't able to do that.

While I was living at home, my first suicide attempt was at the age of ten. I overdosed on Tylenol and was in intensive care for a week. Another time I overdosed by taking a large bottle of aspirin, but I just bruised a lot and bled a lot when we had sodomy. But I thought of suicide constantly. As a child of five, six, seven, I felt very close to God, but later I thought that I was damned, and that broke up my spiritual relationship, which was a terrible loss. I felt that I was a terrible person for not dying to preserve my virginity like the Catholic saints did, because by the age of ten I knew what virginity was and that I wasn't one, and that meant I wasn't a worthy person. That was a very traumatic insight for me, and one that I couldn't cope with very well.

When I moved to my uncle's house, I started attending high school, and a boy sat next to me and stared at me all week long, and I felt under tremendous pressure. At the end of the week he asked me out to the movies, and I said yes, because I did not know how to say no. I had no sense of boundaries. He took me to the movies and he kept his distance, and from then on I was his as far as he was concerned, but I did not know that until much later on. From then on at lunchtime, I was surrounded by his friends from the firehouse, because he was a volunteer fireman— teenage boys could do that back then. I did not realize that they were keeping track of me and protecting me for him; they were very loyal to him. If I went on a date with another boy, he would show up no matter where it was, because his friends would tell him about it. I didn't consider him a boyfriend because I was not emotionally connected to him, but he felt I was his property. Whoever I was with would get up immediately and leave, and I would never hear from them again. He had that kind of presence and power. He was the son of rich people, he drove a hot car, had credit cards, lots of cash, and he owned me, and I could not get rid of him. I would try to break up with him, but I would walk to school, and he would follow in his muscle car the entire way there and back, for weeks. Eventually I would give up and get in the car and reconcile with him and accept his dominance.

His parents always wanted a daughter. He was extremely disrespectful to them, very ungrateful, and I was both respectful to them and appreciative of them; I felt very obligated to them because I was very much a pleaser. Over the years his mother and father became the only parents I ever really had. I married him at nineteen because I didn't know what else to do, and I couldn't get out of it. He wanted an impromptu wedding—his parents wanted a big one, but instead we messed it up by calling our friends on a Thursday night and saying, "What are you doing Saturday? We're getting married." The night before the wedding, I was sewing hems on dresses my mother had made for my sisters out of dishcloths. My father-in-law basically paid twenty-five thousand dollars to my father to buy me. They used the money to buy a house in upstate New York and move the family out of the slums of Jersey City where we lived. My husband continually reminded me that I had been bought and paid for and that my family would never miss me because there were so many other children. My one wish and desire was to somehow pay my in-laws back so that I could buy my freedom, but I had no way to do that. I worked for them, I ran their office, and I took care of all the administrative work for the business for them. They put me through college to get skills for that, although originally I had wanted to go through the diplomatic service.

I stayed with my husband for thirty years, during which time he got increasingly violent. He was also financially irresponsible. His parents basically supported us because he spent money like water on toys, so I felt even more indebted to his parents, and more enslaved, but I remained faithful. One night I decided that I wanted to have a child. My husband and I were not often sexual or affectionate, but I approached him and he was agreeable. Every time he would have sex with me, he made me feel very dirty. We would have sex maybe five times a year at the most for the first five years, and after that, none. But I was lucky that one night, and I conceived that night, and had my daughter. I raised her practically as a single parent because my husband wanted nothing to do with a child. I depended on my in-laws to be surrogates, to help me with raising her, to be the father and mother that I was not able to be. At this point in time, I was becoming more and more suicidal and depressed, and the mental illness was really kicking in.

I hurt my back for the first time when my daughter was six months old and had to lay on the floor for two weeks while my in-laws kept my daughter. I used a urinal and had a bucket next to me to empty the urinal into, and it was agony just to do that. I was not able to move off the floor of the living room. I was not able to pick up my daughter until she was two years old, so she spent a lot time of time on the floor with me. I didn't really think of my child as my baby, although she belonged to me. She felt more like a little sister to me until she was about eleven, and then I started to feel motherly toward her. That disturbed me tremendously, that I couldn't bond with my own child, but my mother-in-law and father-in-law were extremely attentive to her, and lavished everything on her.

My daughter never gave me any trouble; she never challenged me, but in the beginning I was abusive to her. I would take some of my anger and frustration out on her, but she was very forgiving. When I got older, I explained to my daughter that I was fully responsible for my actions; that she was not guilty of anything, and that she never did anything to deserve what I had done to her. I am almost sixty now— I'm fifty-nine—and I continue to work on my relationship with my daughter, which is much closer now. I continue to re-emphasize that I was the responsible one, that what I did was wrong, and that it was unacceptable.

I had numerous mental breakdowns that required hospitalization while I was married. I stayed in that abusive relationship because I felt that I deserved what I was getting. I had very low self-esteem, and I felt like a failure. I was constantly suicidal. I did not live a normal life. I lived under the protection of my in-laws when they found out that my husband had put me in the hospital again with a beating. I finally confessed to my father-in-law what my husband was doing, and he got very angry with my husband. At that point, my husband stopped physically abusing me, but he didn't stop mentally or emotionally abusing me. He threatened me with guns, threatened to kill me, and then the next day when it was over I would get flowers. People thought that he was so in love with me because my house always had flowers.

When my father-in-law died of cancer, I lost my protection. When my mother-in-law died a few years later, I lost everything. By that time my husband was stockpiling guns and ammunition, but I didn't know how much. I told him to lock up all the guns so that I wouldn't kill myself with one, which he did. When he targeted my daughter for abuse and knocked the bathroom door in to argue with her, I stepped in and called the police and demanded that he leave the house. We got an order of protection, which he answered by serving me with divorce papers. At the time I didn't know that he had no grounds for divorce. I did, but he did not. I told my lawyer, "Give him everything he wants." When they arrested him for domestic violence, they confiscated eighty-four high-powered rifles and thirty-three thousand rounds of ammunition, including hollow-point bullets, although they didn't find his pistols, as he had hidden them. The police were upset that they didn't have a space big enough to hold it all, so they had to rent a warehouse.

I told my lawyer that my husband had threatened to shoot me on multiple occasions, and had even shot our dog on the kitchen floor in front of me. He'd played Russian roulette, stuck the gun in my mouth and spun the chamber, and I felt convinced he wanted to kill me. I instructed my lawyer to get me out of this marriage as soon as possible. My daughter was married by then, and I went into hiding with her and my son-in-law for about six years. I got on disability and that bought us food; we stayed with family members for as long as we could, and then would move on. My daughter and son-in-law had hidden some of the possessions that were important to me in a storage area, and when things settled down, they let me know about it. I hadn't known that they could be so generous, to look after my interests in such a way. In the thirteen years we've been divorced, he's never spoken with my daughter, or had anything to do with her. I still live in fear of him.

I've been fighting mental illness in varying degrees of severity since the divorce. The trauma of my life split my consciousness and gave me sixteen multiple personalities, which aid me in coping but are very unpredictable. I never met a person who made me feel loved or cared for until I met Railen; I had slaves that were very devoted to me, but there was something very special about Railen. And in spite of everything, I was still dominant. I was always dominant in every other part of my life except for my relationships. With my husband, I was a prisoner, and I was property, but I started having slaves on the side during my marriage. I didn't have sex with them, because I wanted to stay disease-free, and to remain faithful to my ex, even though he didn't deserve it. But with the advent of the Internet, I started actively looking for submissive partners.

At what point in your relationship with Mistress Thorne did this all come out?

Railen:

There were details that came out here and there, as far as the history of abuse, and later on the history of incest. Just before Mistress came to live with me, she had a breakdown while she was living with the other co-dominant, and I think that was the first one I saw.

Mistress Thorne:

I started going to therapy again. I had been out of therapy and off medication for several years, but I had to return and seek psychiatric help.

Railen:

I think at that point we were already becoming rather close. My motivation was just being there for her, and doing everything I could to help her get through it. I felt protective of her, like I could really be a healing force in her life. It's the panther in me.

How do you make the M/s work through this, and for it? If there are times when you're out of it for any reason, how do you make it function in the face of everything.

Mistress Thorne:

Well, we have some challenges right now. I don't like to be touched. I can be hugged and cuddled, but I have difficulty with sexual touch. I also have difficulty with sleeping at night. So those are two really big problems. Railen suits me sexually, because I am able to pleasure him as I desire, which gives me pleasure, although when he is allowed to pleasure me he is extremely talented, like no one else I've ever been with. I like having no pressure on me to have sexual contact in ways I don't want, but I also know that he has needs. His sexual needs harmonize with my lust for power, and I do lust for power. So to have sexual power over him works for us extremely well. It allows me to deal with my personal sexual challenges of being touched sexually and intimately at a slower pace, without any criticism or resentment, and I feel enabled by Railen to meet his sexual needs in a way that he feels very satisfying. So while I am exerting sexual power over him, I am also getting my power needs met. It's like a compelling and relentless force within me that I need to get met on a regular basis.

Railen:

I'm very service-oriented, so my motivation is not necessarily being dominated. Outside of the bedroom, when it's everyday life, it's my pleasure to serve her, and I get a lot of enjoyment out of it. When her back was out, I was pleased to do things for her. When she's not at her best, I am happy to be there for her. I get a great deal of personal satisfaction out of that. It actually gives me opportunities to be at my best. It's a particularly good fit that way as well. I don't crave the "humiliate me, dominate me, make me feel like a slave" stuff.

Mistress Thorne:

It just seems to happen very naturally and very organically. Railen has a pledge that he recites to me daily, and I'd like him to recite that for you.

Railen:

With my honor, Mistress,
   I freely give my humble gifts
   to the one most worthy to receive them.
 I surrender to you my body for you to enjoy,
   and let your power strengthen and tone it.
I commit to you my mind for you to challenge,
   to let your wisdom shape and hone it.
I promise to you my heart for you to hold,
   that your love may fill and lift it.
I submit to you my power to add to your own,
   to let your will capture and harness it.
And I dedicate to you my spirit,
   to accompany you always,
   to let your essence warm and brighten it.
O Mistress, I freely offer you these gifts,
   honestly, openly, and willingly,
And I pledge to you my service, my obedience,
   and my unconditional love and devotion.
There are none before you,
   and there are none above you.
You are unlike all others, and I love you.

Mistress Thorne:

I am so humbled when I hear this, and so honored. Railen honors me. He blesses me. I treasure him.

What advice would you have for people to find ways to serve a dominant who is currently in a position of needing a lot of care? How do you keep the power dynamic going through that?

Railen:

Quite honestly, there are times when being in service to Mistress requires that I mother her. It's not the natural order of things; it's not what I desire, but there are times when I'll say, "Let's go have some *us* time," when we'll just go in the bedroom and shut everything out until she comes down from whatever state she's in. She'll resist, because she doesn't want to come down from whatever state she's in, so I need to be persuasive and insistent, and stronger than she is at the moment to say, "No, this is what you need! Come on, work with me, let's do this together. Meet me halfway. Come to the bedroom. OK, you don't want to come to the bedroom, just take my hand. We'll take it a step at a time." All I do is in service to Mistress.

Mistress Thorne:

Ordinarily I have a very strong drive to be self-sufficient and self-reliant. I never feel that I'm a lousy dominant, but I've learned humility. Our relationship is more egalitarian than authoritarian, and that forms a bridge that helps me be who I need to be, and helps Railen be who he is and who he needs to be. One driving force within our relationship is that Railen provides me with an opportunity to explore and express my dominance. It's very important to me to provide him with opportunities as well, to explore and express his submission. But also being husband and wife does color our relationship a little bit. There are areas where I respect Railen as an equal in the house by nature of him being my husband, but that does not mean that he bosses me around, or gives me orders. It's just that certain major decisions I will defer to him, if I don't feel equipped to make them. I rely on his strength, and in his strength he serves me. He is a very powerful slave, very capable and a leader in his own right. I require him to be active in the community, which he is and always has been. I feel that it's important for his needs to be met, either by him or by me.

Railen:

We have a couple of mantras that help us get through tough times. First, "Just because things are this way today doesn't mean they're going to be this way tomorrow." It's just that everybody has cloudy days. Sometimes it rains, sometimes it snows, you just have faith that tomorrow isn't necessarily going to be a rotten day. Second, "The Universe provides." The Universe always brings you just what you need, and while you don't always agree or know why for a long time, but the Universe does bring you what you need. And the Universe has brought us together.

Mistress Thorne:

So we try to feed our relationship with things like involvement in our local MAsT chapter where Railen has been an officer, and we associate with lifestyle people,

people of like mind who feed and support us in our lifestyle. We're not islands unto ourselves; we think participation is important. Giving back is important.

What are some of the things he does on a regular basis to keep you on an even keel?

Mistress Thorne:

Well, he reminds me to take my medicine. I'm still resistant in that area. Some meds I don't mind taking, but others I'm resistant to. I don't like having to submit to taking to ones like, for example, Valium. I don't like taking it. But it does cut down on the number of episodes. It provides me with enough of an awake and alert state that I can function better.

Railen:

So I'm able to remind her, "Well, you know that you do feel pretty good when you take it." For the Klonopin, the best I could say was, "Well, you know that you won't feel as bad when you take it." Another thing is being her companion and providing some routine and schedule. I leave for work around 7 in the morning. I get up at some point before her, take a shower, and then I'll wake her up and make her breakfast, and then I'll go to work and she'll either get up and start her day or crawl back in bed, depending on how she is. But we have that moment of connection in the morning before I go off.

Sometimes when I'm driving home from work, I'll notice a particularly beautiful sunset making the clouds light up with that gold-red-pink thing going on. I'll call her and say, "Have you looked out the window lately?" And she'll look out the window and we'll share a sunset together. It's good to enjoy things that are bigger than both of us.

Mistress Thorne:

Our other mantra is "Showing Up For Work". This is an ongoing process, something I can't afford to slack off on. I need to go to therapy, I need to take my medication, and I need to deal with finding a balance between rest and activity. I'm making more and more progress in that area, but I feel it's important for me to be a good example and "show up for work", even though Railen financially supports us and goes off to work every day. My part of the deal is continually working on my problems. But I've made a tremendous amount of progress since I ran away with Railen. My whole life has changed. It's a diametric opposite to what it was like before.

Railen:

I have to remind her how much hard work she's really doing, and I honestly feel like she works far harder than me. The work she's doing and the issues she's working on are much harder than what I do all day.

What advice would you give to someone who would like to be in a position of dominance, but is afraid to get started because of mental illness issues?

Mistress Thorne:

Get rid of that thought. I don't allow myself to have that thought. I don't consider my mental illness to be a detriment to my dominance. I am a dominant. That is who I am, what I must be. Whether I'm sick or well, I'm still a dominant. I'm a warrior; sometimes I'm a wounded warrior, but I'm still a warrior.

Railen:

It's not a coat she puts on or a badge she wears. We were talking earlier about weekend-style D/s relationships. If your relationship with someone is constrained—they're going to come over for several hours once a week on Saturday night, or once or twice a month, I think you can do the "I'm going to put on my dominance hat now," and be dominant for this person so they aren't disappointed. But if you're really dominant, someone can come into your house for the weekend, and you just continue to be yourself. It's who you are. So this would be a significant challenge to somebody who needs to be cast in a role, to put on the costume of a dominant when they're not feeling that way.

We spend so much time together that I have no doubt that even at her weakest, she still feels dominant inside at the deep core. Whether she is feeling like acting on that at the moment is another story, but tomorrow is always another day. There have been times over the years when she's said, "I have plans for you when you get home from work," and then when I get home she's asleep or not feeling well. I'm not bent out of shape about it, because I know there will be another day. When people have just the weekend thing, they're coming over Saturday night and this better be good! It really does put a lot of pressure on people, and that would be challenging.

What about submissives who are looking at a dominant who has mental illnesses?

Railen:

This is about two people coming together to have a very intimate relationship, not a casual buy-a-dom thing. If I was coming over to someone's house and paying them two hundred bucks to dominate me, I would expect them to be dominant. I wouldn't expect them to say, "Well, I just don't feel like it tonight." But when you're actually invested in a relationship with somebody else, they are a person. They are human. Being able to accept whatever they can offer you as an opportunity for yourself to be better, that's a wonderful thing. Whether it's "I'm going to take as much as I can on the St. Andrew's Cross," or trying not to pass out when she's sticking needles in me, or holding her when she's feeling weak, or telling her again that I love her and I want her to feel that, or reminding her to look out the window when it's beautiful outside, or showing her the birds in the yard—these are all ways that I serve her. I enrich her life with my service.

So I'd encourage the submissive to find their strength in this service. I have the mantra, "All I do is in service to Mistress." Everything from taking care of her to being a corporate drone, so we can have this nice house and do things we want to do. Another thing I'd underscore is authenticity and integrity and being true to who you are, finding someone who respects you for that, and making a partnership out of that. We've done very well at that!

Mistress Thorne:

I don't do anything to change him. I like to challenge him, but I'm not interested in changing who he is, intrinsically. And he doesn't make any demands on me to change intrinsically. He accepts me just the way I am.

Railen:

If nothing else changed, if she had these same problems for the rest of her life, I would still be committed to her. I'm not with her because I'm thinking, "Well, we're going to get through this and it will be better later." You can't go into this with your fingers crossed behind your back, or wishing you were with somebody else, or "If only we can make it to this point we'll be OK."

One of the first conversations we had was when I met Mistress at a munch. It was just before a play party at their house. Up until then it had just been BDSM play—she'd given me my first public flogging—and really introducing me to the scene. So she sat me on the couch next to her and got out a big sheet of paper, and asked me to name all the four-letter words I could think of. So of course I started with some of the dirty words, and then the simple ones like Love and Hate and Hope, and we made a huge list of fifty to seventy worlds. Then she put down the pen and we started going through them, and each one was a talking point. "What does this mean to you?" It was her way of getting to know me and helping me to know myself.

Mistress Thorne:

We're going to grow old together. I think it also makes a difference that I am very other-oriented. I'm very giving to Railen and my other slaves, and that helps it to work for us. It is vital to me that Railen be authentic. Not that he fits into a cookie-cutter image of what I want, but that he blooms into who he is. Seeing his progress and growth and development has been a tremendous source of excitement and wonder for me. I am so proud of him.

Railen:

And I am so honored to serve her. Always.

Walking on Barbed Wire: Childhood Abuse From the Dominant Perspective
Raven Kaldera

(The original version of this piece was put up on the Internet in 2008. Those parts are not italicized. The italicized bits are later additions for this publishing.)

In July of 2008, my slaveboy and I went to the Master/slave conference in the DC area. It was Friday morning, and we were sitting in our hotel room, scouring the program for which workshops looked the juiciest for each of us. I noticed a workshop by a slave named Alia on dealing with abuse histories in M/s relationships, but I dismissed it. Actually, it was the last thing that I wanted to go to. The very last thing. Nope, not even thinking about that, totally the bottom of the list. When my boy brought it up, I said so. Vehemently.

Well, he thought he'd like to go. Why? It wasn't his problem, after all. (I'd not read far enough down the description to see those words, "...and partners of...") He reiterated that he'd just like to go, unless I really wanted him elsewhere. It was at this point that I realized that I was reacting out of fear ... and I don't like it when fear controls my choices. I've been training myself for my entire adult life not to react from fear, and to walk toward it whenever possible, so I gritted my teeth and said, "Well, then I'll go with you."

Slave Alia told a long and fairly horrific story about an incredibly abusive stepfather as the opening to her workshop. At first it was all fine—I was just listening to someone else's story, awful as it was. Then she began to describe an episode of abuse that involved her being tied to a towel rack in the bathroom and beaten, and my whole back and neck went into a rigid spasm. My boy, who had his arm around me, felt me turn into solid steel and hugged me in support. Later—he is a massage therapist—he worked on me four times during the day, and the tension wouldn't leave. It wasn't until I allowed myself to remember what memory that story had triggered that the massage began to help and I could start to relax.

My parents were both quite mentally ill, and quite violent. Most families have an abuser and a weak enabler; I wasn't so lucky. Both were equally brutal; I believe that they wanted to abuse each other but were too well matched physically, so they took it out on the kids. Sometimes one parent would hold me while the other would beat me, and then they would switch. Sometimes the abuse would get sick in a way that I have only seen since in consenting SM scenes. Sometimes the people I'd tell, later, about what happened to me wouldn't believe it. I finally ran away at the age of seventeen, old enough to survive on the streets and unable to take any more.

At any rate, one day when I was around nine my mother had a particularly bad psychotic day and tied me to the shower rod in the bathroom by my hair (I had very long hair at the time) so that my toes were balanced on the edge of the tub. She put a paper bag over my head and beat me. I knew that if she knocked me off the edge of the tub I'd be hanging by my hair, so I held my entire body rigid as steel ... and I did not fall. I clung to the porcelain with my toes and managed to last through until she lost interest and took me down. When Alia retold her story, my body flashed back to that moment. I thought I'd worked that all through, that I'd dealt with it. (That's a fun side effect of abuse histories; just when you think you've finished with something, it comes back for a final cameo.) Well, my mind may have dealt with it, but my body apparently didn't get the memo. (That's another fun side effect—dissociation from the body. It can take decades to fix that one.)

While Alia's workshop was excellent in many ways, it was told only from the point of view of a submissive. When someone brought that up, she apologetically admitted that she could only speak from her own experience, and hadn't thought about how things might be different for a dominant. Later, a handful of the dominants who'd been in that workshop (and weren't there just to support their abuse-survivor submissives) clustered in the hallway and compared scars, as it were. It got me to thinking about how the detritus of dealing with an abuse history are different for dominants; how we have our own unique challenges. It's a different game for someone who's in charge to play with this emotional dynamite, and it takes a different course of action.

One problem is the culture of BDSM itself. Being the sort of dominant that most submissives want is a mixed blessing. On the one hand, it was very good training for self-control, patience, and mindfulness. On the other hand, it was also very good training for isolation, emotional repression, and concealing one's true self. It provides a venue that rewards the dominant for being "stone", physically or emotionally, over and over. Topping—especially the sort of "performance" topping done in public spaces—can be a largely distanced and voyeuristic activity; the dominant acts on the submissive but is untouched by them. The submissive gets their experience and doesn't have to worry about what's going on with the dominant. This dynamic is projected on a day-to-day scale in "ideal" D/s. Dominants aren't supposed to be vulnerable, and they certainly aren't supposed to have the kind of baggage that makes you curl up into a screaming fetal ball on the floor. And, let's face it, many submissives would prefer a dominant who was always calm and steady and who never lost their shit. This sets up a climate where dominants are encouraged to control but never fully deal with their issues.

Another problem is trust. This is a problem for subs too, of course, but it's different when it's the person in charge who is unable to bring themselves to trust. Submissives don't generally expect to have to earn a dominant's emotional trust; they expect to be the ones whose trust is *earned*. It doesn't occur to them that it might go the other way, and they are often taken aback when it is made clear. A dominant who can't trust, and who has not yet developed good self-control, may be such a control freak that they become abusive themselves. This is the ugly side of being a dominant personality who was badly mistreated as a child; like a tormented wild animal, they may turn vicious and become abusers themselves, taking the only power that they know. In fact, I think that this is the usual assumption people make when they put together the equation of dominant + abuse: they'll just become an abuser, and thus they are thrust out of the equation ... because abusers can't have healthy

D/s relationships. The only solution is to eject them, blacklist them, and ideally pry any hapless submissives out of their clutches. Dominant abuse survivors who aren't abusers themselves, and can be trusted with a D/s relationship, must have just gotten over it, right?

This simplistic equation leaves out those dominants who have made a commitment not to be their abusers and have developed the self-control to see that through, but who still have a lot of unresolved baggage. I have enormous trust issues. It is very hard for me to believe that people will not betray me, turn on me, and generally fail me. "People only get one chance with you," one lover said to me. It's not always true, but it's true often enough—they can screw up once, and then my expectations for the relationship quietly plummet through the floor. I may still choose to be with them, but I don't expect to be able to rely on them for anything ... and I can't be fully intimate with them.

Part of the healing process for a submissive with an abuse history is gently being encouraged to be emotionally self-sufficient. For dominants, it's different. Generally, by the time we're old enough to be in power exchange relationships, we've got the self-sufficiency thing down. We're so good at it that we awe people. I believe that I was eleven years old when I decided that I would never need anything from anyone ever again ... and I held to that for uncountable lonely years. If I couldn't give it to myself, I would learn to do without. I told my lovers straight out that I didn't need them, but that they should take that as a compliment—it meant that I wanted them, and I was there by choice and not by dependence. (Obviously, I saw dependence as a very bad thing at that point, at least for me. Some of my lovers didn't take that statement very well, but I wrote that off as them wanting me to be dependent for unhealthy reasons.)

M/s—and especially the process of internal enslavement—was amazingly healing for the trust situation. Here was a human being who was openly willing to be entirely vulnerable to me, to allow me to make them helpless ... and entirely harmless. (An abuser might try to force the helpless/harmless qualities on someone; I knew better. What you hold by force or cunning can get away—after all, I did.

For me it had to be offered willingly, with open eyes.) My boy and I didn't start out to do internal enslavement; it crept up on us, but there came a moment when we had to choose it consciously. After much discussion, we decided to embark on that scary journey together ... and it led me into a place of intimacy so deep that I'd never dreamed I could go there. Once he was entirely psychologically unable to leave or disobey me, I could feel safe enough to be fully open in a way that I had never been before.

But that's only the first step. Building trust is not just a matter of courage, or willpower, the great mainstays of dominance. I have enough willpower to crack walls open, and eventually I ran into a point where it didn't help. It's a great tool in the beginning of the job, but eventually you need a different one. At that point, trying to cure yourself with solitary willpower is like trying to cross the ocean on a sword. You are not a Taoist Immortal, and you and your little sword will drown. It's just the wrong tool. You need something more container-shaped, like a boat. Like a cup. Like the open, willing heart of another.

Part of the problem is that sooner or later, you run into the part of that thorny path that *you can't do alone.* Yes, that's the ugly truth, the part that makes us want to bridle and deny it, but that's what it comes down to: these problems were created in close, emotionally dependent relationships with flawed human beings, and they can only be fully solved in close, emotionally dependent relationships with other flawed human beings. The idea that a sizeable chunk of one's healing is dependent on those flawed humans is enough to make one run screaming, really. But that's the whole point: what's the most frightening? Where there's fear, there's power—because real power is transforming triggers, and that process requires other people to do the triggering.

So what tool did I need? For the longest time, I didn't know. Finally, I came into that safe space in this M/s relationship ... but that was just the first part. The next part was dragging my submissive deep into the ugly guts of my psyche, showing him everything about me that was unflattering and difficult ... especially the parts that I feared he'd dislike the most. That's where the courage and willpower is useful again, but what I needed most was for my willing, open submissive to see the worst of me, and say to me, "I love every part of you, including your monster, and I trust unshakably in the part of you that will never let the monster out." This was the right tool for the job, a tool that I could use to take myself further down the path.

That was an important point of it, right there ... I was still responsible, for myself and for my submissive. My job in this was to use him to help myself, not to sit back and expect his love to heal me. At the same time, it was also my job to make sure that he got his own emotional and spiritual needs met, had my help in working out his own problems, and was not pushed beyond his limits by my use of him as a healing tool. We all know that it's best when we don't break our tools. People say that term with the word "toy" in it, but while my slave might be a toy occasionally, mostly he's something far more serious, because this is not a playful business.

While my slaveboy—and my sub boy as well—make wonderful and compassionate tools for my self-healing, there's another part to the process that I wasn't ready to talk about in 2008 when I first wrote this piece. Masters who have PTSD or abuse damage may find having slaves healing for other reasons. (I'm not going to quibble about the actual definition of PTSD, and who does and does not have it, because there's argument over those lines, and according to some I have it, and some would say I don't.) A slave can be a way to get control over an environment full of triggers, especially around intimate relationships.

For example, I have issues with being touched. There are a cluster of reasons for that, but a big one is my abuse history. I don't like being touched by strangers, or for that matter anyone with whom I am not physically intimate or who is not my child. I don't like being touched suddenly or from behind—I may react with what looks like a serious "startle" reflex but is actually me suppressing a violent urge. My boys know exactly how to touch and not touch me, how to ask for permission verbally and nonverbally, and what's off limits. They know to wake me gently, either with soft repeated words or, if allowed, gentle touch. They know never to wake me up with a yell and a shake, because in my not-awake state I may react with violence, which we'll both regret a minute later. They know to get between me and people who run up and try to hug me, and to interpose themselves instead.

My sex life, as well, is a minefield. Having a slave means that I don't need to worry about finding him wandering around in it, cheerfully and unwittingly setting off triggers. I can have sex when and how I feel like it, utterly selfishly. No sexual activity or context occurs that might set me off, and if I'm in a space where I have to be "stone", or where no sex happens for many days, I can guarantee that my boys will not complain, be resentful, or push me to do anything I am not wholly comfortable with. If I quit in the middle of sex, or if my affect is "off", my slaveboy might gently inquire as to my state, but if I don't want to talk about it in the moment, that's OK too.

Some people might say that it is sad that I need so much control over my physical boundaries, that I can't be "free" with my body. Me, I'm just grateful to have sex that I can actually enjoy.

Right now among spiritual D/s practitioners, there's a lot of talk about the "therapist dominant" who dedicates themselves to helping the submissive on their own path. That's not the term that they use to describe themselves, of course, but it's what the role looked like from my point of view. I use the term "therapist dominant" because many of the terms used to describe this position sound a great deal like the language used to describe the ideal therapist/client relationship ... with the exception of all those sexual intimacy boundaries that therapists aren't supposed to cross with their clients. In these relationships, since an important component of them is the healing and emotional comfort of the (possibly damaged) submissive, the dominants stand back and let the submissive project all their issues onto the dominant, and work through them in that way. The dominant's job is to be the rock that they pound themselves against, until they are through the need to do it.

Make no mistake, there have been people with whom I do this. I call those people *clients*, at least to myself, and usually to their faces as well. They are not my lovers, and I am not emotionally intimate with them, even if I am (in rare cases) sexual with them. I keep firm, wide boundaries between them and my own personal issues. I allow them to hold the masks of their various abusers up to me; I allow them to work out their authority and parental issues on me ... and I keep my own stuff far away. That's done not just for them, but for me as well. Their need to project onto me would conflict with my need to know that they see the rawest, worst bits for what they really are, uniquely and personally. For there to be any intimacy at all between us, I would have to rip off the mask they were trying to put on me, throw it on the ground and stomp it to death, and then rub their face in my own special internal darkness. *This is me. Do you see me? Do you still want me?* If I can't get that, I need to keep them at a far distance.

This is one reason why I strongly suggest that if one half of a D/s or M/s couple has a certain set of issues, and they want to use the other party (consensually, one would assume) in order to work that through, it's best if they do not have the *same* issues. They can both be broken, but ideally it should be in very different ways. If they're both abuse survivors, they can trigger each other by turns. I'm not saying that it could never be done, but both would have to be far enough along in their healing to be able to cleanly put their own stuff aside in triggering circumstances, and that's a hard call.

The reason I couldn't write about having slaves as a way to create a softer, less triggering environment was that I feared doing that. I feared that it was me "coddling" myself, that I ought to be tough enough to take anything and not be affected. The problem with this attitude is that while I repressed and toughed-out, I wasn't actually making any progress. In order to make progress, I needed to be gentler with myself and cut back on triggering stimuli, in order to focus on one thing at a time. (I also needed to do that in order to be any sort of emotionally available to my partners.) That meant carpeting the house emotionally, so to speak, and slaves are awesome for doing and maintaining that carpeting. My boys love any opportunity to make my life easier. I've also proved to myself that I will still attack my issues, no matter how "coddled" I am by them.

The next thing that I need from my slave, in order to do this work, is that he be entirely dependable. Everyone makes mistakes and messes up from time to time, but I need to know that he is absolutely committed to being as reliable as possible. Growing up with mentally ill and violently abusive parents meant seventeen years of never being able to expect anything to be there when you need it. While some people may glorify living without expectations—"Embrace the unknown!"—when you're a kid, and you have no idea from day to day whether you're going to be greeted with careless affection, deliberately vicious criticism, or a crazed, screaming beating, it can put you in a state of hypervigilance. Nothing is certain, including everyone in your life and their various promises. If someone starts acting out of character, bad things are surely going to happen, or so your experience tells you. In order to healthily embrace the unknown, you need to have a firm grounding in reliability under your feet.

That's why this is no place for brats (a type that my boy defines as "charmingly disobedient"), or rebels, or any slaves who disobey out of ennui or needing attention or needing a catharsis and not being self-aware enough to ask for one. It's healing for me to be able to give a command and have a strong certainty that it will actually be obeyed, without a scene, without my having to be constantly vigilant for whatever is going to go wrong this time. It's healing to know that we are a Team, not adversaries. To me, many of the techniques used to extract obedience from disobedient slaves put the master and slave in adversarial opposition. I prefer to know that we have the same expectations of how things are going to go, and the same dedication to making them go that way. To me, when a slave rebels for no good reason, it means that they aren't committed to being part of the Team, they are not reliable, and they don't trust my judgment. And if that's the case, why are they here? I'm not saying that every M-type with abuse issues will have this need, but if you're a submissive and you're dealing with a controlled but wary dominant with these problems, it might be a good thing to keep in mind. It also helps to be patient, steady, and good at not taking things personally.

This comes around, again, to the wounded dominant needing to get to a point where they can be healthily dependent. In order to get to that level, they need dependability. They need to be able to build the safe space that they didn't get. Submissives with abuse issues often look to a dominant to build that space for them; the dominant knows that he or she has to do the work themselves. The submissive's job is to be the tool with which they do it, understanding what that entails. The right submissive is also the tool with which the dominant proves to themselves that they are indeed effective and can have an impact on the world (a state which their childhood told them not to expect), and can be effective in more ways than simply surviving. The submissive needs to be very invested in giving them that experience of effectiveness.

The submissive also needs to be all right with the times when their dominant withdraws and shuts down for a while. (This is where that ability to not take things personally comes in.) Sometimes we're just going to go into lockdown for a while in order to struggle with our demons. Sometimes that's for everyone's safety, and you should be glad of it. Sometimes it can be scary, being left alone out there, but we do come back ... and being dependable means that when we come back, there you are holding the cup like nothing happened.

Here I am talking to the submissives instead of the dominants, but I think I've done a good deal of talking to the dominant side already, and there are probably some apprehensive subs out there who are saying, "I don't know if this is something I want to deal with..." That's a legitimate worry, regardless of which side it's coming from. If you're uncomfortable with getting involved with someone who has deep scars that still make them jump when touched, don't do it. Your eventual inability to be there for them will just reify the view of the world that they are struggling against. Saying, "I am afraid that I would let you down, and I don't want to be yet another one who does that to you," is paradoxically a helpful, honest, and reassuring thing, even when it is disappointing in its own way.

But for those who are willing to faithfully hold that cup ... it's also useful to us when you can show some pride in how willing we are to keep struggling. With all that pressure from the BDSM community archetypes that I mentioned earlier, it's not hard for a dominant to worry that the sub's perception of watching that struggle will be that they are weak. Bother to let them know that you think it's strong to attack that; most people, after all, just go through life with no mindfulness, simply reacting from their damage. Doing hard work on yourself is an exceptional and courageous thing, and proof of character. If you don't believe that this is so, this is not the job for you.

One example, for me, is kitchen timers, of the tick-tick-tick-ding! kind. When I hear them go off, I get nauseous and my whole body clenches and shakes. That's because my abusive mother was an obsessive time management hobbyist, and liked to write up and time her children's day to five-to-fifteen-minute intervals. Lists on the bathroom door detailed how many minutes we had to use the bathroom, shower, brush our teeth, do chores, etc. She would use her kitchen timer to make sure that we were within the time limit, and if we weren't done by the time it went off, she would beat us. To this day, I can't have a kitchen timer in the house.

However, a year or so ago, I did have my slaveboy buy one. I put it on the table and sat with it, and worked on tolerating the sound of it—not because I so crave having one in my kitchen, but because I wanted to see if I could overcome the nausea and shaking. My slaveboy stood by, respectfully waiting in case I needed anything. After a period of trying and failing, I made him pack it back up with the receipt and take it to the store. Maybe next year I'll try again. In the meantime, he does whatever it takes to make it easy for me to have a safe space to continually challenge myself.

Now back to the dominants. I don't pretend that the small scraps I've gleaned about this process are true for every D-type or M-type. They may even be unique to me. However, if yours are different, talk about that. Put it out there. That's an act of courage, baring those scars and telling others how they can start to heal their own. Do it, even though it is even more painful for you, with your history, to show any vulnerability. Do it because if we all just sit there behind impassive masks pretending that nothing is wrong, the next generation of wounded would-be dominants will have no one to turn to ... just as we had no one to turn to, just as we were let down. Let's not keep that cycle going. If you can't speak it face to face, write about it. Let it pass from you somehow, because that's part of the healing.

This is where the real strength is. Not in the ability to bend a submissive to your will, but in the ability to bend those stubborn internal demons, who are just as strong as you are ... because they're made of you.

HEAD GLITCHES: NEUROLOGICAL DYSFUNCTION

Mastering With Asperger's
Master Michael Shorten

I'm a forty-seven-year old master who has Asperger Disorder.

Early in my childhood, around the age of five or six, I remember being evaluated to see if I was "hyperactive". It was at the age of seven that I became aware that I had a hard time making friends. High school was extremely difficult; I had a hard time socially. I still didn't seem to understand how to make or keep friends, or even interact with people. I found computers in the late 1970s, and they became my most enjoyable outlet—they made sense! My fellow students did not. Dating was next to impossible. I felt as if I had missed out on some class or special presentation back in fifth grade that would teach us how to make friends and influence people.

I suffered from depression and anger management issues, and I was eventually abandoned to the state by my parents as an "incorrigible child" after my second attempt to run away. I struggled in foster care situations and eventually became a transient runaway until I was eighteen and joined the military.

During my time in the U.S. Army and U.S. Air Force, I still struggled with social issues, but I did manage to get married, and I eventually left the military to make a career and a life. I still struggled with communication and social situations, but I figured that it was just something I'd never understand, although I never had an answer as to why. It wasn't until I was diagnosed that I realized how much that had bothered and depressed me. It had been the biggest question of my life: why couldn't I be like the people I admired? Why could they navigate socially and professionally while I was as smart, as driven, and as capable as they were? I couldn't seem to figure out the missing part.

As I got older, I seemed to mature out of much of my depression and anger. I did some therapeutic help with some specific issues, but overall my social struggles continued. I had trouble with communication issues in my relationships, both personal and professional. I struggled with understanding people but still just figured I'd missed that mythical class in the fifth grade.

It wasn't until I sat in a classroom with Dr. Robert Rubel and heard him talking about Asperger's and autism that light bulbs started to brighten. I was more interested in what he had to say about Asperger's than his actual topic on protocol! At the time, my interest in Asperger's was to help a young family member who was having difficulty with school and life, and had a great many quirky behaviors. After hearing about Asperger's, I found a way to get this family member into testing to be diagnosed.

The more I learned, however, the more I realized that if I'd been asked the questions that were being asked of this family member, I would have answered in ways that would have diagnosed me as well. I went through the testing process myself, and my clinician gave me the news: I was high-functioning, but I was on the autism spectrum with Asperger's—and also that I had learned about as much about how to navigate through life as I was going to learn without specific help.

In the meantime, I knew that my sexuality was also "different". I'd done all the things that adventurous young boys and men will do as they go through puberty, but my fantasies and erotica always tended to go toward BDSM and kink. The thought of women doing as I commanded, of subjecting them to all of those evil, twisted activities that lurked in my head ... it was always there, but unrealized in any form. I had enough troubles just getting a girlfriend, thanks you my social issues. In 1984, however, I had a couple of experiences that taught me that maybe my kinky desires were shared by others. The first experience was finding mysterious text files on this thing called a BBS. It was erotica written by others and put out in these crude precursors to websites and forums. Wow! Other people thought about the same sick stuff I did? It was freeing to know that I wasn't alone and that perhaps, perhaps, I might even be able to see some of these fantasies come true. Soon afterward, I had an experience with a couple of women whom I connected with as casual sex partners.

They wanted to play "tie me up" games, or have anal sex, or be spanked, or be told what to do in humiliating ways.

Fast forwarding to 1994: I had joined the Air Force, gotten married, and had a daughter, and then I found Usenet through night college—including alt.sex.bondage in particular. Suddenly my kink interests, which had been only masturbation fodder, exploded. Here were real people talking about dungeons and munches and parties and all sorts of things. I took a few years to listen, learn, and figure out what interested me. I went to local discussion groups and munches in Chicago, and attended events and parties at the old Leather Rose dungeon. In the year 2000 I got divorced from my largely sexless failed marriage, and after that I sought out only kinky relationships.

I became about as out as someone could be, getting involved in a lot of different groups and events. The original Galleria Domain was open, as was the Leather Rose located on Fullerton, and these places were like magic to me. The next three years were amazing as my social life became centered around kink. I was starting to learn more about leather and a deeper commitment to a path that had opened up before me.

In 2003 I started a Master/slave relationship with my current slave, angie. We both got more involved in the Leather community and the Master/slave community over the years, and in 2012, angie and I started on a new journey by becoming the Illinois Master/slave for 2013. This would lead us to compete and win at GLLA in August of 2013, so right now we're on our way to Dallas to compete at the twenty-fifth International Master/slave Competition. We've had to really look inside ourselves and each other in this new journey, and our Master/slave dynamic has deepened and become more rich for it.

So how did I become a Master? I had always wanted to be the one "in charge" since I'd started having sexual fantasies. When I first experimented with kink, I tried bottoming once, but it turned into an "escape and turn the tables" scene. I never found an interest in it after that. However, SM activities aside, I found myself drawn to a particular set of folks who identified as "Master" and "slave". I'd met some people who'd called themselves that, but they were either abusive in their relationships or just not what I wanted for myself in M/s. I found only a few people who really walked the talk. I was drawn to them, to how they did things, to how they carried themselves and conducted their relationships. I asked questions. I learned things and I listened. It was a journey that took time, patience, practice, and experience to get to where I felt comfortable pursuing a 24/7 Master/slave relationship.

When someone is "dominant" in a relationship, the way that dominance is expressed depends on the nature of the relationship and the people involved. The way I was taught, a Dominant/submissive relationship is based on control and submission, where a Master/slave relationship is based on authority and surrender. In my Master/slave relationship, I have accepted authority over slave angie's life and she has surrendered to that authority. To quote President Truman, "the buck stops here."

Still, I questioned myself right after getting diagnosed—should someone with Asperger's even be in an M/s relationship? I realized pretty quickly that I had been who I am before the diagnosis and would remain so after. Asperger's was something I've dealt with all my life, not something I'd gotten recently. That meant that I was the same "me" I had been before; I just had a name and a reason for some the challenges I face. I didn't stop being the Master, the person who could hold authority over another. I had already navigated those waters, but now with what I knew, I could probably deal with them a lot more effectively. So now it doesn't bother me at all. None of us are perfect, but what determines if I can be a good Master is about what I do and who I am, not about my Asperger's.

My slave and I have lived in a 24/7 Master/slave relationship for the past ten years. We define the "power exchange" as authority transfer; she's given me total authority over her life. I don't "control" her (except when my Asperger's hits and I go into a micromanagement mode—which I'm learning to rein in—but I do hold the final say and final choice. To the vanilla world, our relationships looks like a loving, respectful, and supportive relationship where she just happens to have a pretty necklace that she wears all the time. Inside the Leather/kink world, we look like a loving, respectful, and supportive relationship where the collar around her neck has much more meaning than just pretty jewelry. I took many elements from what I learned from folks here or took away from classes, and—most importantly—experiences that we've shared together. It's based on authority, respect for each other, responsibilities to one another and the relationship, her service and duty to me, my service and duty to the relationship and our Leather.

The authority part may not be easy to spot, but although angie can (and does) operate on her own, she does it within a set of protocols and expectations that I've communicated to her. You'll see her going about her business, but there are times when she will come to me to ask about things. These are done pretty quietly and smoothly without drawing attention to them. The respect part—I hope—shows in how we interact with each other. We laugh and play a lot, and we don't take ourselves too seriously, but we also don't hide that she belongs to me. I don't treat her badly, and I'm not shy about valuing her, whether it's her input into a conversation or her activities with me or the community. The "service and duty" part—from her to me and from me to the relationship—shows in what we do as she takes care of me, and I take care of the relationship. Our leather … well, that's how we play and fuck, that's our circle of friends, and that's our service back to the community.

The number-one struggle in our relationship, early on, was communication—specifically, how we could communicate in a way that I understood versus the emotional way that she communicates. At first she adapted in a less-than-satisfactory way. She would try to figure out what magic combination of words would work to satisfy me, but this just led to frustration. She would take all the responsibility for getting it wrong and feel guilty about it, which would build up into resentment and cause issues. We'd get past that, but the root cause—my communication is so different from hers—never changed and we didn't understand it.

It wasn't until I was diagnosed that things started to click. Instead of just chalking up our (occasional) big and (more often) small communication glitches to "just us", I could examine the situation and evaluate with a more complete set of facts. Now her adaptation is still communication-related, but rather than struggle with "we aren't speaking the same language", now we work on "OK, what are the words that make sense to both of us?" The fact that we know the "why" of when communication can break down makes recovery and success a lot more easier.

I work best on facts. The emotions get tangled up, either due to high sensitivity to the emotions behind words, or the jumble that I get from neurotypical people when they communicate in words, but their body language says something else ... or worse yet, when I miss the social context. It's not angie's first nature to communicate with just facts, but she's gotten very good at it, and at figuring out how to work all the various angles until it makes sense. My own adaptation has been to count to one hundred instead of ten, give myself more pause, and to really listen when my Universal Translator (angie) suggests to me that maybe there's another way of hearing something. She's also adapted by requesting (and getting) protocols in how to deal with certain situations—for example, if I get into an overload situation, or if I lock down because I have to recharge and empty my mental bucket, or if I require her Universal Translator services.

At this point, I need to go into my Bucket Theory, which I use to describe how my sensory issues work with regard to my Asperger's. (The following essay is copyrighted on my website[1].)

---

[1] http://ourmasterslavejourney.info/2014/01/27/the-bucket-theory/

An Aspie's Theory, Similar To The "Spoon Theory"[2]

Ever since she has been diagnosed with lupus, angie and I have used the "spoon" concept to communicate about her energy and what she can accomplish in a day. Back in December, I was trying to communicate about how stimuli can have different effects on me, as someone with Asperger's Syndrome, and I came up with the "bucket" theory to describe how I see and deal with stimuli.

Imagine that I start off the day with a bucket. I hear something intense on the radio going to work … and a couple of golf balls get tossed in the bucket. As soon as I get in, I get slammed with several problems all at once and folks are getting into my personal space and I am quickly overwhelmed. More golf balls in the bucket. Someone is wearing really crazy perfume and it just assaults my nose. Yet more golf balls in the bucket. I'm asked to do something in a social situation that I don't have a good idea of how to handle. This time, a huge softball goes in the bucket. Then I get home and the granddaughter is visiting and the house is full of shrieking, jumping, running, slamming doors, waving arms, TV is on full blast. Lots of balls, big and small, go into the bucket.

At some point, what's going to happen to the bucket? It's going to overflow and I can't hold onto those balls. I need to do specific things in order to deal with the overflow and overload, so that I can empty the bucket some (or all), come back, and be OK.

Problem is, I don't always have a consistent bucket size. Sometimes it's a huge bucket and I can deal with all the things. Sometimes, it's a shot glass and I can hold only one ball, if that much. It varies with my sleep, my diet, and the amount of stress in my life. It also varies with the balls themselves—the

---

[2] http://www.butyoudontlooksick.com/wpress/articles/written-by-christine/the-spoon-theory/)

size of them or the number of them represent the stimulus of the situation and how much it's going to impact me before I overload.

For me, the bucket represents the fact that as an Aspie, the intensity in how I process stimuli gets to a point where I can't contain it, and I don't interpret things in the same manner that neurotypical people do. That filter isn't there, and situations that neurotypical people can normally handle become very intense moments, especially where I'm dealing with the "social blindness" that I may have in particular situation.

Realizing that I have to be aware of where I'm at with the bucket, and that I'm responsible for taking care of myself, have been huge in my comfort level in being an Aspie. I can be proactive in trying to understand how big my bucket is, and manage myself to that point. I can forgive myself when I need to take a moment (or an hour) and unwind and empty that bucket a bit. I can also look at angie and tell her "Bucket Filling Fast!" and she'll understand, at some level.

Another area that is still difficult for me is feeling comfortable in social situations like I see neurotypical people seem comfortable. It's about being able to pick up on the cues and nonverbal messages that most neurotypical people can manage. It's about knowing what to say and knowing how to continue on a conversation once the facts have been delivered. Those small subtle things have never felt "natural" to me. What I do is to learn from experience, figure out a "path to success", and apply that to the list of programs and flowcharts in my head. ("OK, she just smiled at me. I recognize that smile as a warm, inviting smile, so now I can talk about what is going on, or what she likes about what is going on. Oh, this is going well. She made a reference to what I'm doing, so she might be interested in what I'm about...") My diagnosing doctor says that I have about 75% of the skills that most neurotypical people would have, due to life and age and experience. (I've also learned to use my slave as a

Universal Translator when I want it.) I am now very aware of a person's language, and I'm very sensitive to moods and emotions. I've been learning to better filter that and to recognize my own limits and my own overload situations, when the bucket is getting full.

Before my diagnosis, I didn't handle full-bucket times very well. I would have bad days, and they would sometimes spiral into really bad days where everything I touched exploded. I couldn't communicate at all on those days because I was in such a bad place, and neither of us understood what was going on, so the household would usually end up very tense. A good analogy would be that those were the days that I was the Hulk and not Bruce Banner.

Now, because I understand a lot better about what is going on, I can communicate with my slave that I'm having a bad day, that the bucket is full, or that the communication is going south in my head. She knows to leave me alone when asked, and to come at things differently when the communication isn't working. Fortunately, the communication is much better now, and when it goes wrong, I'm more than likely to catch it first and let her know to come at things differently. (I'm reminded of the movie *The Incredible Hulk* from 2007, with the "293 days since last incident" subtitles. That's probably a good visual for here too.)

My slave couldn't cope well with my bad days before my diagnosis either, because I didn't give her good enough direction or protocol to be able to know what to do. Before diagnosis, my triggers would go off and I wouldn't understand them. Now, I get it, so I can give her warning when I'm in a bad place. Often times, I will leave her in a "default protocol" place (basically, that means to carry on with what she was already doing, take care of herself and the house, and check in on me periodically) and I will give myself some space to empty the bucket. That is at most a few hours, and I come back and we carry on.

If slave angie has questions about what I've told her to do, she respectfully communicates with me. She'll ask for permission to voice her opinion. She has found ways of getting me to realize when I may be compromised in my process. I would say that since my diagnosis, I've gotten very good at knowing about my own ups and downs, and from what I see in her, she trusts me even more now because of it. Overall, angie trusts me because even on my worst days, I've never made a decision that put us in danger or compromised our relationship to the point where her trust was broken.

Service is a huge component of our Master/slave relationship. One of angie's required services is to be my Universal Translator. If I am not sure of an email, or if someone acts in an odd way and I'd like a second opinion on what I'm seeing, if I'd like a second set of ears to hear what I want to say to someone, she provides that service for me. She is very happy to do it, because it is a very direct way of making my life easier or more pleasurable. I've made sure to put the boundaries in place so that it doesn't become a "needy" type of dependency on her—she knows that I turn the Translator on and off. My Master/slave relationship is about the authority I have over her life and the control I have over myself. She provides me with that service because it is what I want and require from her.

Angie started reading about Asperger's and autism when we were getting the diagnosis for the family member I spoke about earlier. She continually reads forums and articles, especially about NT/ASD couples/partners. There was nothing specific that I've found she's had to learn in terms of a new skill—it's been more about tweaking her communication and understanding to take my specific issues into account.

My advice to an Aspie master would be to learn what overloads you. Understand your triggers and stimulus reactions. Feel comfortable making mistakes and not getting what a neurotypical person would get, because you are you, and you are a unique miracle. Cultivate a friend (or partner or spouse) who can help be a sounding board or Universal Translator. Read books on Asperger's and autism.

Learn what you need to feel safe, to get to places of understanding in communicating with neurotypical people, and learn how you can best empty your own bucket. Be patient and forgive yourself; you are not a bad person, you just have different wiring. It's probably made you very smart and very skilled in unique ways. Embrace those.

Understand that if you are with an neurotypical slave, you can have them serve as a Universal Translator. Establish some boundaries and protocols to keep the right power exchange or authority in place. Establish protocols and default behaviors for when you have bad days or bad moments. Make sure to reconnect after those times.

If you're the slave of an Aspie master, or you're considering an Aspie master, learn about Autism and Asperger's—what it is, how it affects someone, and how it affects this master right here. There will be good days and bad ones. Don't be afraid to ask for and work out the protocol for when your Master has a bad day. And be patient! Communication with an Aspie master may be more difficult, but it can be done. Don't be afraid to go to some sort of counseling/therapy to learn better communication skills, if need be. However you need to visualize it (as a social colorblindness, or something similar), recognize that this is how your Master is wired, but it has made that person into the unique and wonderful individual who is very much worth serving.

Dominating On The Spectrum
Kate Shea

I'm Kate, and I'm twenty-six and I have a hard time with labels. The only thing I can say for certain of what I "know" would be accurate on my label is that I'm over six feet tall and I have blue eyes. Oh, and I am what I hear is a "ciswoman"; I think it just means that I came in sporting a vagina. However, the only thing I know for certain about my vagina is that I was born with it.

So I guess I'll go with ciswoman; I can't find a different word I fit with. I can't say I'm always "fem" because sometimes it's fun to be a "boi", but I'm really tall so I suppose I could always butch it up, or put on some lipstick and make myself a Glamazon. Can't I just be me? I have a hard enough time trying to figure out what I am by other people's standards without taking what jingles my girl bits into account.

I own my boy, but am I a "Proprietor" or "Dominant"? Am I just an environmental control freak who's a complete bossy-pants and won't accept not having her way? Really? There's an attractive way to word that? "Domina", eh? I like that ... But what about the sadomasochism thing? Well, apparently I can't do both. Really? I like to make people scream and cry, I like to hurt them and push them and see what happens. I could spend hours rolling around in the glory of turning my pet into a pile of boy-goo. That makes me tingle. But wait, I can't hand the boy whatever evil implement I choose and direct him how to use it so I can have my catharsis ... because then I'm not in "control"? Um, you caught the part about *handing* it over and *directing* the situation, yes? Is that too hard to bend your perception around?

Well we'll have to try to make it easier for you, so now we have to define the boy, or should we call him sub/slave/property/pet/service top ... uh oh, we'd have to pick all those apart too, and that doesn't lend him a physical label, just a placecard.

Apparently it has to be this hard.

Sexual preference? Pansexual/Polyamorous.   I appreciate the "I love the person not the gender" sentiment, but please, there's a percentage of us that need to get honest here, it's not that we love the inner you in some holier-than-thou-twue-acceptance. It's that no matter what you are, you attract us, you're sexy and we'd like for our sexy bits to have a fine howdy-do. Is there a label for "My Horny is Non-Discriminatory"? (Because apparently "indiscriminate" just sounds skeezy.)

These all seem like creative ways to label what could be perceived as personality flaws or obsessions, putting them into pretty packages so that everyone else can "understand" what we are, and what we do. What's wrong with some mystery? What's wrong with some communication? If I could put myself on a card and have you understand it, oh, believe me, I'd be throwing them at everyone who passes me. Maybe if I sharpen the edges ... that'd work...

So ... Hi. I'm Kate, also known as Nyx. I'm over six feet tall, I have blue eyes and I came in sporting a vagina. This is my pet; I own him and I love him. Beyond that, call it whatever makes sense to you.

I feel like the metaphorical onion. I'm lucky that I'm wickedly intelligent and have done a *lot* of work to understand how people's emotions work. On the outside, I can put on a roguish awkward charm that utterly disarms people, and I can be conversational and well spoken and make everyone feel special. In that exact same instant, me on the inside is saying Oh my gods, what are we doing?!

I was diagnosed with Autistic Spectrum Disorder in my early 20s. It went wrongly diagnosed for years before that. My mother is supposedly bipolar (something I will argue till the end of her days), so they assumed that I was the same and started feeding me medication. There was no talking, therapy, counseling, nothing. If someone had actually really sat down with me and listened, I bet we could have figured it out sooner. I have always had sleeping issues but they gave me an anti-psychotic as a sleep aid and it made me incredibly suicidal. I overdosed on it at least 3 times (I have huge memory gaps from the time I was medicated, annoying because I usually have a steel-trap memory) never once did my parents catch it. All three times I essentially "slept" for four days and they just assumed I was depressed and didn't want to be bothered. I still wrestle with myself to forgive them that.

The final straw in the medication was an appointment where I spent the whole appointment saying "I'm not taking this crap anymore," but they wouldn't stop bothering me until I took the prescriptions and stopped arguing. I filled them that day, and put them in my drawer and didn't touch them again. Fast forward to my appointment six weeks later; my mom races into the office saying how wonderfully I'm doing and how "You're brilliant, I have my daughter back!" and this is the best thing to happen to our lives. At which point I pulled all the dated prescription bottles, full, out of my pocket and put them on her desk. My mom was shocked, the psychiatrist was shocked. I said "If no one is going to listen to me, I don't need to be here" and walked out of her office. I remember my mom screaming at me the whole way home but I have no idea what she said.

Now I don't take any medications, beyond a multivitamin and a heavy dose of a B-complex (it seems to lessen the violence of my nightmares) and fibre; I'm gluten intolerant and sometimes the way I eat doesn't always make my colon happy, so I supplement it. I have an "as needed" prescription for migraines, but they aren't as bad as they were before I stopped eating gluten. I'm about to go see a surgeon about a uterine hysterectomy since the dehydration of my chronic periods seems to aggravate my migraines as well, and I straight-up want no children.

As an adult, I discovered BDSM. I found great catharsis in masochism and believed that the only way I could achieve this was as a slave, I felt enough "out of the norm" that I didn't want to challenge "the way things are" in kink. I now know there are plenty of sadomasochistic dominants, but at the time I believed that my obsessive need for control and structure meant I should be under someone else's structure, so that I wouldn't fret so much about it. All these attempts utterly exacerbated all my issues and made me a miserable person. I love to dictate schedules and routines, and my structures are logical and make perfect sense (at least to me), so why shouldn't I use them to run a whole house?

I'm naturally a bossy-pants, and keeping control of a situation lets me structure it to remain as functional as possible. I also find that when you carry a "capital D", people are far more inclined to give you personal space at events. I'm 6'1 so I can be somewhat intimidating, and I'm not going to lie—I do use that to my advantage to keep people in a respectable bubble so I don't feel crowded. No one argues with a big scary D-lady when she says "Out of my way, I need to go outside *now*." The crowd parts and I can trot through with no issue.

I'm a total control freak, and I have to be—my autism gives me so many sensory problems that I can waste too much time and energy coping with them otherwise. As a dominant in our relationship, I can monitor my environment, the stimulus, the routines. I can have the last word on what decisions are in the house and feel like I'm initiating the change which helps me get through it more easily. I'm the one who decided that our four-legged pets were coming into the house. He now sees just how functional they keep me, and where before he didn't understand why it was so important to me to have dogs and cats and fish in the house, he gets it now. I also like that being dominant gives me the ability to dictate when/where/how/if I'm touched. I enjoy that my control of our activities gives me the ability to say "No, we're staying home, I can't do that today." I also decide what kind of car we drive, and I can edit his driving habits if I don't like the rhythm he uses when he pushes the gas or brake.

I love that I get to make final decisions about *everything*. Pet can't buy clothes without me, because I have tactile issues and I have to make sure I'm okay with how the clothes feel before he can purchase them. This also applies to all the fabrics in the house... the sheets, the towels, the washcloths, the dish rags, the dish towels, the rugs, the door mats, the car mats, the blankets, the curtains, the blinds, any wall hangings, sofas, chairs, table clothes, placemats, napkins etc. As a dominant, it's very easy for me to say "I don't like how that feels, we're not getting it," or "I love how this feels, we *have* to get it." He makes no assumptions that he can decide what I will or won't like the feel of, and waits until we can do those things together. This also applies to music choices, ambient temperature preference, how heavy the blinds are, any scented items in the house, personal hygiene products, cleaning products/methods. I make colour choices about anything that comes into the house, I have some colours I really don't like, and some I strongly prefer. I don't have a room in my house that doesn't have something red in it, because red helps me "reset" my brain when I stare at it.

Most see this as micromanaging but we're both so in the habit of being that way no one else notices. He just looks like the most caring and devoted boy in the world who always thinks of me first. I like that he's very charming and gallant, well mannered and chivalrous (though our version of "chivalry" is motivated differently and often used to appease my dislike of touching strange things like doors or drink trays).

I am reliant on him financially. We had a long hard talk about whether I was going to keep trying to work, or if we were going to follow medical advice and have me leave the workforce. I recoiled at the idea of being a "housewife", as the very concept angered my inner feminist. However, I don't really do any of the "housewifey" things. If I want to, I'll help clean, but it's not expected. I like cooking; I'm good at it, and I've been able to work on really complicated time-consuming recipes since I'm home to supervise the kitchen. I get to pick and choose what I feel like doing throughout the day, or if I just need quiet time I can have it. I work with the dogs (one is a "vicious" case that I'm still working on). Sometimes I freak out that I'm useless and broken, and Pet will usually remind me of all the things he does in a day because I've given him orders. Sometimes I feel a bit like a regent, in that that there's not really a lot for me to do except have fun and ensure my regency is happy, until the shit hits the fan and decisions and judgments need to be made. Then I feel indispensable.

My two very short-lived vanilla relationships in high school failed because they touched me too much, and they expected me to understand all these smooshy "feelings" that I don't have. It was kinda doomed from the get-go. Because I sometimes shut down verbally and have a hard time articulating what I'm thinking if I'm feeling stressed or intimidated, I was downright miserable in the couple of relationships where I tried to be on the bottom half. I can't answer a stream of questions if I'm having a meltdown due to sensory processing issues, and the verbal assault tends to aggravate it more. I seemed to pick people with "assumption-itis", and they would attach their own reasoning to why I was having problems. At that time I didn't know I was ASD, and had no words for it, or ability to explain myself. I felt ashamed that I wasn't normal in so many ways, and any effort I made to describe it was accused of being "crazy" or "stupid" or "oversensitive", which just made me try to hide it more. I ended up very angry most of the time.

I met Kyle (Pet) on October 20, 2008, and we've been fairly inseparable since. We moved in together on August 2009 and eloped on February 25, 2012. Having the words now to explain what my issues are, and having someone who very obviously adores me (and would run through hell and back for me), has made being functional a much easier process, actually. I've taken great pains to try to understand myself as best I can, and I've done just about everything that I *can* do to learn how to cope and communicate. I've put in an awful lot of work—and still do—just to be able to make things go along as smoothly as possible, but it seems like everything I deal with is a double-edged sword. The ASD gives me distinct advantages and disadvantages in every situation. I'm oversensitive to sensory input, so it's very easy for me to "read" of Kyle's energy level and know where he's at without having to actually ask. I know him well enough by now to know what his particular "buzzing" means. It can also mean that his happy-go-lucky bouncy self can grate on me if I'm having a bad day. My sensory problems, which heavily dictate which items come in and out of the house, may keep clutter to a minimum, but they make it very difficult when we *need* new sheets.

I'm often told that I'm the "most functional" autistic person anyone has ever seen. Sometimes I think people forget that it's still every bit as hard; I just make a practice of trying to engage. It is always an interesting experience when someone sees me on a "bad" day for the first time, and suddenly the reality of the amount of work I put in to function for short periods in normal society becomes apparent to the outside observer. I have to be careful of the environment I'm in, and often I have to ignore things to get through the situation. I don't generally go out without someone I trust present. The only places I go on my own are the store downstairs in my building, and sometimes the chiropractor and my doctor, but only to my family doctor. If there's a "new doctor" situation, someone comes with me.

I developed a lot of coping strategies that are good at concealing the ASD, but unfortunately they do me a disservice when it comes to being functional and taking care of my own needs, so I'm working on changing a lot of those. It is hard to change habits; ASD people hate any change even at the best of times, but I'm seeing the benefits of it. I'm making better choices for myself, and I'm trying to engage with Pet in a way that promotes understanding, where before I tended to retreat. He is *very* understanding that I can't always explain something in the moment but will come back to it. We've had a lot of really awesome conversations from it.

I've learned not to make life-altering decisions unless I'm in a good place. That's part of why the big step of me leaving the workforce became such an in-depth discussion between us; we both knew I wasn't in a good place, but it seemed like the only way to get back to a good place was to leave the workforce! It was one of the hardest decisions I've ever made, and some days I really regret it because I don't like having to rely on someone else, even him. Most days, though, I feel honoured that I have someone who is willing to support me. I use that as a source of confidence—someone thought so much of me that they chose to devote their life to my security and comfort!

Decisions made in bad moments are all made with the intention of getting to a better moment. Over time we're becoming more efficient at communicating when I'm not in a good place, and he doesn't take it personally when I use words too literally or say unintentionally mean things to convey a point. He knows now that it's not about him, and when I am in a bad place he has become extremely proficient at changing his tone of voice so it doesn't grate on me, and asking short 'yes or no' questions to establish what I need. It's always a work in progress, but we choose to work on it together rather than letting it separate us.

Pet has done a bit of research on ASD, but never assumes that what he reads is the be-all and end-all, because he knows it looks different for everyone. Something worth mentioning here is that Kyle has ADHD/OCD, so he's very understanding of what it's like to exist with something you can't do anything about. He is adamant that I do the things that make life better for me—he ensures I get to medical appointments, makes sure I've talked out all I want to talk out, and drags me to the chiropractor because he knows that when I'm in pain I have a harder time with sensory processing. He knows a lot more than he admits to, but I don't think he focuses on "Am I doing this to make up for her shortcomings?" It's just part of the job he does to serve me—not because I'm defective, but because his presence enriches my life and makes me feel a lot better about myself. When I try to pull back and look after myself (because sometimes I get indignant about having to rely on him and throw a temper tantrum), it's very obvious that it hurts his feelings. It's not just that he hates when I look at myself in that way, but it also robs him of his purpose and leaves him feeling lost about what he's supposed to do. I never thought I wanted a service slave until he morphed into one!

He's nicknamed my "pit-bull" because he's a devoted loving man (albeit with a good dose of cocky sassy-pants, which I find very endearing), and he assumes responsibility for my security as a guard dog would. In the same way that a Great Pyrenees or Akbash or Anatolian Shepherd would be left with a herd in the mountains, or a Karelian bear-dog would run after large game, he's in his element when I need his service. It gives him a sense of security to see that he can do so much toward my functionality. It gives him a job and a clear-cut life goal. He relishes knowing exactly where he fits, and is happiest when we're doing things together.

I know that some days I am difficult, and he gets tired and frustrated with me. He is often forgetful, so if I'm not in a place where I can direct him, things will go undone, which can sometimes become a downward spiral. Sometimes when that happens, I say "I'm going for coffee," and I'll go see one of my nearby friends. This has become a cue that says "Get some shit done around here, so I can come back and see that you've accomplished things, and feel more comfortable in my environment, and we can get back on track." I do have a hard time when he is gone due to having extra work to do, and I feel like it's my fault because I'm not working, and I resent it. At the same point, his working so much keeps him out of my way a lot. I don't need the same kind of interaction neurotypical people do, and I often appreciate the independence and alone time.

There are lots of things he has to do because I can't due to sensory processing problems. For all that I can disassemble dead things into dog food, I can't squish spiders; they crunch and it's gross. I also can't re-level the gravel in the fish tank cause I scream bloody murder when a fish touches me. I like fishing, but he has to take my fish off the line. I can gut it once it's dead, but live slimy wriggling fish are not okay. When we're doing things together, some things have become such an easy dance that I just assume he's going to be there. Other people are charmed and entranced by it; it's very sweet. For example, if I'm standing and holding a mug, he'll see me take a sip of my coffee and instantly be at my left hand to take it if I haven't got somewhere to put it down. This is because he knows I talk with my hands and have trouble holding a mug level. Little moments of service like this have come to have deep meaning to us.

Both he and I would say I've totally rewired him. For example, I'm a horrible sleeper and he can sleep through anything, but he's had to learn to wake up more easily because he snores. It's a sound I can't deal with, and it makes me want to punch him in the head, so he needs to be able to figure out quickly that I need him to roll over before I go crazy. I'm either completely heartwarming or a complete boar in the morning, so he's learned to tread lightly. Don't mess with the morning routine, and don't talk to me until I start talking, unless it's to say "Coffee?" Better yet, don't ask—just bring coffee.

I will have days where I freak out and cry and stomp and throw things, and I need him to be calm no matter what if I start getting wound up. If we're having fun, great, but I need him to recognize when I'm clearly becoming overstimulated and give me some kind of cue to chill out. I don't have many meltdowns anymore, now that we know what to look for to keep it from happening, but sometimes I become neurologically overstimulated and they just happen. He has to learn to decipher my situation from whatever words I can give, and sometimes just my body language. (That's difficult because it's not always congruent with how I'm feeling, but usually if I'm trying to hit him it means "Get out of my bubble!") He has had to learn to go against some of his own nature, as he's a very protective man and tends to want to instantly enfold a crying person into a hug. However, that is sometimes the *worst* thing to do for an ASD individual who is having a meltdown. He's had to find ways to meet his need of being in physical contact with an upset person that works with the moments when I can't bear to be touched. Silly as it is, sometimes that means he sits on one end of the couch, and I sit at the other and smack my foot on his thigh. To a lot of people this behavior would look like the standard "cheeky S/M" situation, with the dominant teasing the submissive, but it's really not. It's not motivated that way at all; it's more like Reiki or other energy-work—I'm literally driving out my negative energy through another person. When I'm in a good place where I can actually enjoy S/M for what it is, that's a great way to mete out extra excitement for me too.

I tend to come across as very cold and calculating; I've been described as sociopathic by medical staff who didn't understand how differently ASD individuals express emotion. I don't have a lot of emotional complexity. I have a very dark inner self somewhere, quite like Dexter, if you will. My father was military, and I learned their code of honour, and I abide by it. I sometimes have to deal with very strange thoughts inside my head, and even though he completely doesn't understand them, he's not scared of them either. However, he's had to unlearn and relearn a lot of things he thought he knew about "all women". I don't fit that at all—ASD individuals often don't absorb social gender cues and expectations well—and he loves me for it now, where it baffled him at first. Gender fluidity was a very odd concept to him at first, which confused me as I apparently had to learn that not all bisexuals are genderfluid.

We have an unspoken code to monitor how I'm doing when we're out somewhere. If an event is loud and I've decided that I'm staying on the patio, he will immediately hop to, making sure he brings out everything I might need. Then he gives me space and pops in and out at regular intervals, telling me what's happening inside. He looks very attentive and charming, which he is, but it's for different reasons than most people might think. He knows that if I look at him quickly multiple times it means "Get me out of here." If I look at him and smile, I'm fine. If I look at him and raise an eyebrow, I need something. If I look at the space next to me, it means I want him to stand there. When he's next to me, I use him as my "tuning rod". I stay very close to him in new situations, so he can silently signal me if I'm being overly "odd". I've learned by now that I can trust him with anything.

If you're a submissive looking to settle in with an ASD dominant, you will need patience and a sense of humour, and especially the ability to find levity in awkward situations. It's also good if you have a common set of goals. Establish the non-negotiable points quickly, because they aren't going to want those to pop up later after you've reassured them that it won't be a problem. Some of my quirks are neurological and I just can't change them; if you can't deal with them, we can't be partners, and it's better that we figure that out quickly. They say that you shouldn't discuss religion or politics or sex or family on the first date because it isn't tactful; well, I lack tact, so they tend to be some of the first things I discuss. I like knowing a fairly complete picture of a person as soon as possible. I have "files" about people in my head, so don't be uncomfortable when it feels like an interview. It is, but that's how I roll.

The advice that I have for a would-be dominant with ASD is to be as blunt, honest and up-front as you can be to potential subs. Yeah, you're going to freak out a lot of people, but you'll save yourself a lot of time and expended energy in the end. I went into my relationship frank and open from the get-go about everything I could find a way to explain. I found someone willing to work with that, and I didn't waste time. I figured out who I could and couldn't trust very quickly from using one or two granules of honesty as a litmus test to see what they could handle. Cold? Maybe. Smart business choice? Definitely.

Explaining yourself to people is much easier with media being what it is now. I explain myself as "Sheldon and Amy's offspring experiment" from The Big Bang Theory, or the Yoda/Bruce Lee/Chuck Norris of Awkward. There are documentaries that give people a visual on how things about me work. I have a lot of reference material I can use, without throwing textbooks and medical journals at people. Is some of the media negative and unfair? Yes. But at the same time, even the bad stuff gives a "normal" person a starting point you can explain from. I used a National Geographic special called "Test Your Brain" to have a conversation with one of my friends about how my brain works versus how his brain works.

It's worth it to build yourself some social skills before shopping around, even if you're looking for someone who won't care if you don't have them. In some circumstances, the idea of "fake it till you make it" with regard to social skills isn't necessarily a bad one; you'd be surprised what good habits you can instill just from repetition. I've become skilled at being warm and welcoming to new people at munches, largely from forcing myself to do it frequently. I'm complimented often on being charming and welcoming, skills that I have *zero* innate ability for but have built out of consistent trial and error. I have a very small group of trusted people, and anywhere I go, one of them is usually with me so I have a monitor for other people's actions. By watching the reaction of my trusted person, I can adjust my perspective as needed, and understand when people are over- or under-reacting. It's handy, because I know they won't steer me wrong and have my best interest at heart. (Perhaps this is why most of my friends are submissives!) Some ASD individuals have obsessions, like trains, maps, video games etc. My obsession in particular is people; how and why they tick. This is perhaps because I am obsessed with learning, and people are by far the most complicated subject ever.

I was an only child, and my parents' chosen parenting attitude was, "Whatever it seems she needs to learn, we will teach it." I was always encouraged to be curious and ask questions; if I didn't understand something, I could always ask no matter how odd it seemed. When I was small I indicated no empathetic understanding of body language, so my mother assumed that meant she should teach it to me. We played the "Faces Game", a role-playing game where we would practice making and guessing facial expressions and body language. For example, my mom would cross her arms over her chest and scrunch her face up, and taught me that meant "I'm angry, or you're in my space and you need to back off." I learned that other people had "bubbles" too, and didn't necessarily want me inside of them any more than I wanted them inside of mine. They took great pains to teach me social niceties (my mother came from a good family and my father was a high ranking reservist, so I needed decorum and manners from a young age), body language, how to interact, how to have a polite conversation, and many other things.

My father taught me how to describe things by rote process. He would have me describe an action, such as "How do you tie your shoes?" verbally, in great detail—go to where the shoes are, figure out which shoe is left and which shoe is right, figure out which foot is left and which foot is right, remove laces from inside left shoe, loosen tongue of left shoe, slide left foot into left shoe toes first, make sure heel is inside shoe not on shoe, pull tongue of left shoe straight ... and on and on through the process. It was tedious and frustrating, but it taught me how to be verbal and how to describe anything to anyone. Some of my friends say I'm their "translator" between how I see the world and how they do, which is perhaps why it's been easier for me than for other ASD individuals to create understanding in those around me.

It's *not* easy, and I never pretend it is, but my obsession says that it's worth it. I think that's why I like Kyle—he's so animated and talkative that I don't have to exercise my brain much to know where he's at, because he'll tell me. He knows by now to just say everything and I'll ask questions. If I need further explanation, I'll call one of my other trusted sources and say, "If I said 'verbal spew here' to you, how would you feel about it?" The people in my circle take what I say at absolute face value, strive to not take my words personally, and strive to thoroughly explain their reactions. It's complicated, but I feel like I expand my brain working on these things.

Interview with Lee Harrington
Lee Harrington (with help from his girl Butterfly)

Lee:

I am an individual who has been identified as being "strong but psychologically fragile" by a therapist recently, something that really resonated with me. Things that are considered normal "life hiccups" in the world at large can affect me on a disproportionate level to others, and my perception of those things do not always match the experiences of others who share those experiences.

Labels are great conversation starters, but challenging when they become door-closers. My mental adventures are not just challenges, but blessings as well—something I have to remind myself of on the hard days. Part of what gives me challenges has also given me a great capacity to compartmentalize, and to put on masks on the hard days. I can put on a great stage face to be able to operate in the world at large … until I can't.

As for my classical demographic details: I am a thirty-four-year-old man with a female history, having gender transitioned at the age of twenty-six. I was diagnosed with temporal lobe epilepsy in 2001, and have lived with both neurological challenges and non-normative mental health much of my life. In 2012 I chose to dive into a year-long immersive mental health program as part of my journey into strength for the future.

I became a part of the public BDSM community in 1996, and have lived in this community ever since. I'd explored kink with partners for two years previously. In those two years, parts of my exploration were (in retrospect) abusive. In my (pre-BDSM-community) desire to explore dominance, I was told that to be a dominant meant that you had to suffer in non-desired submission to whatever a dominant partner or Master wanted, in order to earn the right to be the dominant. Coming into the public kink community taught me that submissives are allowed to have rights, dominant partners do not have to be perfect (or assholes), and that diversity in desire is the spice of life.

In 1998 I began teaching classes for friends (and keeping a kinky sex blog), and combined this over the next few years with working as a kinky adult film actress, photographer, website owner, and bondage performance artist. Kink, BDSM, Leather and all other sorts of sexual adventures are now my full-time living, including teaching sexuality topics at the university level and writing books on the topic.

Dominance is something that I have embraced in both play and in my lifestyle. I have been honored to have individuals that have had a diversity of identities (Boys, Girls, Slaves, submissives, Property, Puppies, Ponies and more) who have been in service, submission or surrender to me. But who my dynamics have been with do not equate the entirety of my dominance. I find that being dominant is about harnessing a part of my core and delivering it to the surface and my connection with myself, my partners, and the world. I do not consider myself "a dominant" per se. I consider dominance to be a part of my being, and that I have opportunities to have that part of myself be a guiding light in parts of my life.

Butterfly:

Although my behavior would suggest that I have been kinky for most of my life, I did not find the BDSM scene until after I divorced in my late 30s. We came across each other, and it felt like we had always known each other and we always would. I had no way to explain my desire to be of service to him or to be at his side. It did not seem possible, given our life situations and dynamics, that we could be together; but our life opened the way for it to be an option to be in a 24/7 relationship, and we stepped into those roles naturally.

We have been together for about a year and a half now, and our relationship is very fluid and multi-faceted. It goes from traditional power-exchange to feral, to ageplay (one of our favorites is role-playing an 80-year old couple), to what probably looks very vanilla to the outside world. The most consistent titles we come across is Sire and Lady, which allows me to step in when needed to assure that my Sire is cared for, successful, and ready to do his best work in the world. That role does not interrupt my humanity, much less my need to be cared for, successful, and ready to do my best work in the world. It is simply that by being of service to him I am *more* cared for, *more* successful, and *more* ready to do my best work in the world. It nurtures my soul to be useful to him.

Lee:

Attending a class on Earned Leathers at Southwest Leather many years ago, Master Archer was asked by someone about how she could ever be worthy of the cover her family said was hers. Master Archer argued that you do not earn your cover once. You earn the right to be wearing it every time you put it on. Thus, dominance in Leather community and within relationship dynamic is earned each and every time. Sometimes I succeed, and sometimes I do not do so to the level I desire or expect of myself. It is a quest towards a part of my own greatness.

There was a period of over a year that I found that I could not, in all honesty, don my leather cover/cap. If it denoted my Mastery, and my capacity to rule with rightness of heart and action, my mental challenges and emotional fragility got in the way of that rightness. I have had periods where I have been erratic and unable to live up to my obligations in dominance, and where I have been unable to receive the service I have stated I wanted, or was unable to see that it was being given.

I have painted a story that dominant partners must have their life together, be consistent, and be able to follow through on their word. I still believe that, but there was a time when I could not deliver on those things based on my mental health challenges. Healing is not a straight line, but I am somewhere more solid than where I was, and my dominance is now something I can come to with more solidness and honesty.

Previously, I would isolate and only hold my dominance to light when I was capable of it. I would often prevent those in submission to me see me from the worst of times, and come out just for a weekend, just for a week. I'd keep that piece of my authentic self visible, and not let the rest come to light during those times. That was not sustainable with the reality of what was bubbling on the other side of the jewel of personal experience, and as such, my expression of dominance was not sustainable.

There were other times where I used my emotional deregulation as an excuse or crutch, expecting partners to "cope" and "deal" with it, and telling them that it was simply a part of me. This colored my dominance, how my partners interacted with me, and my wellness in the world. Looking back, I feel that both my partners and I deserved better, but I could not see it at the time. I can, however, move forward with growth in mind, choosing to not have my challenges define me. I can choose to move through challenges rather than having them actively hobble me and my relationships, even when times are hard.

Butterfly:

There are a variety of ways in which his disabilities can manifest themselves. Most commonly it is when a small stimulus of daily living disrupts his stability and his ability to be a fully functional person. One example might be him having a panic attack at a conference dinner, and my job was to gently and quietly put him in a safe place so that I could go and get his medication. Another example might be noticing while I am driving that he is not his best self, and pulling back from the conversation so that he has an opportunity to re-compose himself.

At these times, I will silently consider the main point that I needed to make, and let him know, "When you are available, I would like to get back to discussing our financial agreements." Doing so is almost like putting a bookmark in the conversation. It is interrupting the flow, yes, but it allows us to both come back to the topic when we are both at our best. An important part of this is making sure that we are dealing with things one at a time, rather than letting topics stack up. Through early interruption, we are able to catch issues when they have gone "sideways" in a minor way, rather than letting them build up and majorly disrupt our life, stability, and joy. Though this can be challenging, it is an act of service that I offer him.

I think this is not dissimilar to a study I once read by John Gottam about how couples were asked to interrupt fights if either's heart rate went above 190, and not return to the conversation until a half hour after heart rates normalized. We use Dr. Glenn Siegel and Mary Pittman's

The Values Based Model, which includes (1) open honest direct communication (2) respect for self and others (3) responsibility for one's choices (4) accountability to others and a willingness to hold others accountable (5) inclusion of all members and all parts of self; as a base model for how we relate to each other. This allows for ground rules of how we interact with each other if either one of us is faltering.

Lee:

I have found comfort in a Daddy/Sire space with my partner, with whom I also have a complex relationship as a partner first and foremost. Instead of establishing our relationship as *only* one of these facets, we have chosen to enter into a life as partners, seeing how each of our parts interact with the others. She has come to my Sire as my Lady, submitting to me as her Lord, but strong in her own right to the world at large as the Lady of our house. We have so many ways we match up that it has allowed us to dance through my challenges and hiccups. When a Lord has a hard day, the Lady steps up and manages the home. A queen has power in her own right, and can manage the affairs of the king, without shame. When I am in a place of fear or pain, her answering a text message for me or stepping in on projects is not her taking from *me*, but adding to the success of *us*. Her doing this work that was originally mine is a continued form of service, even if it was not one we originally planned.

However, it's not pretty when I am in a space of pain, distance, or emotionality, and it's not acceptable to be there in the long run. Part of our power exchange together is her service of offering me advice, offering me resources, helping me get to my appointments, helping me process challenges. These are a form of service, a form of power that she grants me. I have days where I feel unable to put on my leathers, own my power, feel able to get dressed in a way that is "acceptable" to go out to a party. I have times when I have been convinced by the negative stories that run through my head and rattle me deep, including ones about my worthiness to be in partnership, or how damaging I am to anyone who would want to serve me.

On these days, any form of relationship or play feels so beyond my capacity that I shake.

The tool of "fake it till you make it" has been profound, which includes playing dress-up. I ask my partner to choose clothes they want to see me in. I go and grab ropes. I focus on them and their bodies, rather than thinking about me—a form of mindfulness where only their responsiveness is in my mind. The pain falls away, because all I see is them. Our connection, our play, and their belief in me provides a platform from which we can erotically and energetically soar.

Butterfly:

Our protocols include daily systems, such as having him choose my lingerie each day, and having me bound to our bed each night, which allow us to stay connected. The stability of daily practices maintains our connection even when we have difficult times or are drifting apart. The values-based model encourages me to speak openly, honestly and directly when parts of me are uncomfortable or concerned, and to include "negative emotions" so that they can be ironed out or woven into the greater story of our relationship.

I only try to connect with the sliver of wellness, no matter how large or small, that someone has available at the time. Connecting with my sliver of wellness that I have available at that time, and bringing it to the table as well, creates the utmost success between us. I know that I can work to expand my sliver of wellness, though it will naturally ebb and flow based on my state of nourishment, restfulness and health. I know that I can create environments where another can expand their sliver of wellness, but I cannot expand it for them.

Safety is a core need for both of us. If that is not being experienced by either of us at any time, the dynamic of Sire and Lady allows me to step in to the service of both of us to assure safety. During the worst-case scenarios—the times when he has walked away and I was unsure of his safety—I had to detach with love, deeply grounded in the knowledge that I did not cause his mental illness, I cannot control the mental illness, and I cannot cure that mental illness … but I do have choices around the mental illness.

(This is based on an Al-Anon slogan.) For me personally, because of my own issues of PTSD, safety is an important concept. I've used EMDR and the concept of a "safe place" to help me understand that as an adult I have the capacity to seek and create safety around me. It can start with a meditation, literally redecorating my cluttered mind while settling and addressing the different needs of all of the different parts of me. (For more on that concept you can visit www.dnnsinstitute.com/media/M0/index.html —a psychotherapy model for healing childhood wounds.)

Lee:

I encourage people with fragility and mood adventures to create safe spaces where it is okay to just be. We have a temple/play space where I can go and meditate, and a garden that is ours. I can tell her I need private space, and she respects that, because she knows I will come back to her needs as soon as I can—that my dominance is held with integrity behind it, even if a hiccup has come up. I encourage honesty in the days where it is tough, even if it is cloaked it words that hold dynamics in place. "You are *mine*, and because of this I need you to do this for me." "Yes, Sire, because I am *yours* I will do this."

In doing this, it is of profound importance to me that the person who is in service to me knows the difference between serving in hard times and being abused. I now ask people what their "walk-away" line is. What is too far? When will you walk away if I cross a line? If people don't have one, I can't have them serve me. I do not like the idea of anyone accepting being abused by me on days I don't see my behavior. My behavior is not an excuse for poor behavior, especially if it is said that mental health challenges are the reason. Personal responsibility, on the part of *all* parties, is key. Saying "I was having challenges and that's why that abusive behavior happened, that's all," is unacceptable. We have agreements of "walk-away" level behaviors, and a requirement of personal responsibility and regular personal growth on the part of all parties. When we have a hiccup, we will discuss it within a few days, and "Please ignore that it ever happened!" is not acceptable, especially within the framework of power exchange.

Butterfly:

Service is a privilege that only comes after having taken care of my needs. If I am not fully fed, feeling safe and nurtured, I cannot provide the service that I would like to provide for my beloved. If I start to resent service, it is an indication that I have not put on my own oxygen mask first, which is required before I can help anyone else.

Lee:

We are each in service to each other, and to the relationship. That is part of power *exchange*. It is a collaborative creation, and ideally everyone thinks they are getting the better end of the issue. However, that's easier to say on good days. On the hard ones, when hiccups happen, it doesn't always seem that way. It's taken us the last year of us focusing only on each other to figure out systems like me agreeing to walk away and call within an hour rather than hurt her to the quick when she is in a place of service. We stumbled, it hurt, and we found systems. But it took her having hard lines, and me being willing to figure out the next step with her.

We have customized each other through building a life together, therapy, bouncing off ideas with friends, many hours of interpersonal dialogue, ritual work, and more talking. But beyond the talking, it has been profoundly important to implant hot scenes and consistency into it all to. I choose, ever morning, what lingerie she wears. I tie her using rope to the bed each night. Especially when it is bad. Especially when it is bad. It helps root us, ground us, into the stability we both need.

To a dominant who is working through their issues while trying to be in charge, I'd say: Breathe. Remember to continue with your exercise, mindfulness, artistic outputs, therapy and other programs to build consistency. Find spaces to share those systems with your submissive or service partner so that they can support your success and understand what you need for that success. It might not *look* like a specific need is a big deal, but if the understand it, they can help make your grounding happen.

Laugh. Breathe. Stop comparing yourself to others. Let them tell you why you are an awesome dominant, and actually listening. Tell them they are amazing, with full presence and heart. Check yourself on how often you are saying "yeah, but". Go get your dick sucked (or whatever hot play you like), and include your D/s play in it, not just what you need to make your household work. Listen to what they need. Listen to what they want. Let them help make it happen collaboratively. Say thank you. Say what you appreciate, specifically, not just a general thank you. Honestly apologize, and say what for, rather than blanket reflexive apologies. Take time to apologize to yourself, and forgive yourself.

Fantasize. Take a long walk. Eat something delicious. Let them serve it to you, or prop your feet up on their back as you eat it. Find sexy ways to make little things that can be hard be better. Listen to your needs. Share them. Listen to their needs. Make sure to repeat back to them what you understand their needs to be. Sometimes, we can turn something our submissives say into more of a "fact" than they in fact are.

Take your meds. Go to your appointments. Work to be a better person. Don't let your neurological or neurochemical non-normativity be an excuse to be rude, cruel, or unjust. They deserve better, and so do you.

Butterfly:

I think both partners need to be committed to doing the internal work before entering into a relationship with an honest appraisal of both their strengths and their weaknesses. What helps them be able to do their best work in the world. Both parties must acknowledge that no one is going to fix you, but when a relationship is working right, it helps create an environment of nurturance that allows you to continue to grow. It is important to realize that, as human beings, we are never done growing, changing and evolving. Once you think you have it all worked out, the dynamic may change, and may require real-time adaptation. Realize that the fantasy of dominant or submissive needs to include the reality of both of their human capacities, frailties and needs.

On further thought, answering these questions might seem more like general relationship advice rather than hot, sexy, kinky BDSM advice—but our play often gets complimented, and what I try to explore is the underpinnings for that play. On that structure I believe you can hang any sort of kinkiness that you are into. Our play just happens to involve a lot of rope, power exchange, energy exchange—and we enjoy it a lot. We hope that each of you go out and explore your authentic kinkiness with a partner who does so as well, and that you follow your bliss.